THE ENDURANCE

FACTOR

For foreign and subsidiary rights, contact the author.

Cover design by: Sara Young
Cover photo by: Kim Graham

ISBN: 978-1-960678-77-5   1 2 3 4 5 6 7 8 9 10

Printed in the United States of America

THE ENDURANCE FACTOR

How ministry leaders can avoid burnout, live well, and finish strong

GREG SURRATT AND CHIP JUDD

AVAIL

DEDICATION FROM GREG:

*I dedicate this to my mother, who taught me
well, the principles of resiliency. Thank you
for your long talks that healed my soul in the
midst of normal teenage angst. Thank you
for your encouragement when I wanted to
give up when I felt like a failure at ministry.
We only had thirty-four years together. I miss
you every day. I think you would be proud.*

DEDICATION FROM CHIP:

*Thank you, Pastor Greg, for inviting me
into this project and generously sharing this
opportunity to influence and impact the lives
of leaders, their families, and their organizations. You've succeeded where others have
failed. I'm honored by your friendship.*

CONTENTS

ACKNOWLEDGMENTS

FROM GREG:

Thank you, Chip, for coming into my life and introducing me to the Father's love. I will be forever grateful.

Debbie, you are the love of my life. For forty-seven years you listened patiently to what must have seemed to you like crazy ideas and dreams.

To my four kids and fourteen grandkids—some call it chaos, we call it family. It's the best kind of family. We've learned to love each other well.

To the churches I served and the teams I've led, you've shaped me in ways that were painful at times and helpful always. I'm not sure I would've changed a thing.

Thanks to Martijn and the team at Avail that put up with Chip and my (mostly Chip's) timeline.

Here's to living well and finishing strong.

FROM CHIP:

Thank you, Coleen, my awesome wife of forty-seven years, without whom I would not be who I am today. I love my life with you!

Thank you to my super cool children and their spouses for succeeding at their #1 mission in life—giving us grandchildren! (Just kidding.) I am honored to be your father.

Thank you to all of my friends who have encouraged, poked, and prodded me to write. I thank you for your patient endurance. Here are a few names that come to mind in my almost fifty-year journey: Phillip and Lynn Miles, Murray and Brenda Presley, Mark and Robin Merritt, Rod and Char Reid, John and Lisa Bevere, Doug and Jean Jones, Boodie and Nadine Walters, Ed and Barbara Dickerson, Thalia Vincent, and the awesome people of Victory Christian Fellowship.

A very special thank you to Pastor Fred and Jan Denham. It's because of your obedience that I am on the track I've been on for these forty-seven years.

CHAPTER 1

THE DAY MY WORLD TURNED UPSIDE DOWN

GREG'S TAKE

On Thursday evening, May 7, 2020, I was sitting at dinner with my wife Debbie and a couple who are friends in our neighborhood. My cell phone buzzed in my pocket. The caller ID said the call was from Amy Patrick, the wife of Darrin Patrick, a close friend who had recently joined our staff team. Darrin and Amy hadn't moved to South Carolina yet. They were still in the St. Louis area. I thought it was strange that Amy was calling me. I'd only gotten a few calls from her since Darrin and I had been friends, so I immediately anticipated that something terrible had happened—I didn't know how terrible, but still terrible. I answered, and Amy's first words were, "Darrin's gone."

I got up from the table, excused myself, and stepped outside. I asked, "What do you mean 'he's gone'?"

Amy told me, "I think he's taken his own life." She said, "I think" because, at that moment, the cause wasn't completely clear. Darrin had gone to a shooting range with a friend, and Amy didn't know if his death was an accident or a self-inflicted gunshot.

Darrin had spoken at Seacoast the weekend before. He and I had talked on Tuesday, and I could tell he was very sad and depressed, but we'd also talked just a few hours before Amy's call to brainstorm about a message series we were planning, and he seemed perfectly fine. This happened in the middle of the Covid shutdown, so getting information was very difficult. It took some time, but the medical examiner concluded that Darrin's death was suicide.

Darrin was a terrifically gifted speaker and leader. He was one of the founders of the church planting network, *Acts 29*. As the pastor of Journey Church in St. Louis, he led the church to amazing growth, and it had a powerful impact on the community. But the stress of pushing so hard took its toll. In an interview several years ago for an article by Leadership Network, Darrin described at least some of the symptoms of burnout: "In addition to stomach problems and not being able to sleep, I couldn't concentrate. In fact, I usually read to gain insight and encouragement, but during this time, I couldn't focus well enough to read. I used caffeine and sugar to keep my engines going. On top of all that, the joy of serving God turned into a burden. It was a dark time."[1]

Like many pastors, the stress of the job was greatly compounded by emotional and psychological damage inflicted during his childhood by his father. Darrin hadn't seen strong and loving leadership in his father, and the imprinting of his dad's attitude and behavior began to infect his leadership. On multiple occasions, the elders of Journey Church raised problems of his lack of self-control, manipulation, domineering attitude, and misuse of authority, and his avoidance of a suitable response led them to add another flaw: refusing to be accountable for these serious flaws. After a long and difficult process, he was removed from his position as the pastor of the church, which devastated him.

Darrin asked me to be his pastor, and for two years, I led him through a process of restoration. My love and respect for him grew during that time as I saw his tender heart and genuine repentance. At the end of that time, I asked him to join our teaching team. For a while, he flew from St. Louis to spend a week with us, preach on Sunday, and then fly back. In March of 2020, Darrin and Amy made plans to move to Mt. Pleasant. Their oldest daughter was a student at Liberty University, their second daughter was finishing her junior year in high school, their son was about fourteen, and their youngest daughter was about eleven. They planned to fly in to check out schools and

---

1   "Creating a Culture of Balance," *Leadership Network*, 2006.

sports opportunities for the kids, but the week they came was the week the country shut down to stop the spread of Covid. They determined that they needed to wait a while to make the move. I assured him that we were committed to his family and God's timing. Two months later, Darrin spent a week at Seacoast, preached on Sunday, and flew back home. That was the week he died.

The news of his death shocked our staff team and the people in our church. They loved Darrin, and they marveled at his speaking gifts. The next day, on Friday morning, two members of our team flew with me to St. Louis to see Amy and the kids. We were just about the only people on the plane. When we got to their house, it was filled with people who love Darrin and Amy. Almost every face was wet with tears. It was one of those awkward situations when nobody wants to be there but everybody needs to be there. I quickly realized a lot of plans were still up in the air. I wanted to help Amy take the steps necessary for the funeral, so after a few minutes, I asked Amy and the children to join me and the others who had come with me in another room. We talked and cried. I then spent some time alone with Amy to help her sort out the decisions that had to be made.

All of us leaned hard into our faith in God, but He gave us the freedom to ask the hard and unanswerable questions, at least unanswerable on this side of the veil: "How could this happen?" "What could I have done to prevent it?" "What signs did I miss?" "Where were you, God?" "Why didn't You stop this?"

That night, the three of us who had traveled from Seacoast went back to the hotel. I felt terribly lonely. Part of it was that we were the only three people in the huge hotel; but far worse, my friend had left me without giving me the chance to tell him one more time that I love him. I'd held it together all day, but in the room that night, I sobbed uncontrollably. My grief was compounded with the realization that Darrin, Chip, and I felt called to help pastors deal with life's difficulties, but I couldn't even help my own friend.

> **He gave us the freedom to ask the hard and unanswerable questions, at least unanswerable on this side of the veil.**

Because of Covid restrictions, Amy couldn't have a normal funeral, and the people of Seacoast couldn't gather for a memorial service. A mutual friend, Brian Carpenter, called to invite me to join some other pastors who needed to grieve the loss of our friend. From all over the country, about a dozen of us traveled to a farm in Kansas. For a couple of days, we shared stories about Darrin, we cried, and we laughed. It was a healing time together.

THE ENDURANCE FACTOR

Somewhere in our conversations, I shared the dream Darrin, Chip, and I had shared, but I'd lost my vision for it. Who am I to offer help to pastors when a brother I love killed himself? A couple of the men pulled me aside and gave me encouraging, prophetic words that God was still in the dream, and I shouldn't give up.

Two months later, I received an email from a businessman who offered to donate eighty acres of land near Charleston for a retreat center for pastors. He asked if I was interested. I'm not sure how he knew about the dream, but I told him, "Yes! I'm definitely interested." The property is just outside Kiawah Island, and when I saw it, I was blown away. It's beautiful! I spent the next four months getting input from the trustees at Seacoast to see if "free" was really the deal it seemed to be. It wasn't. Marshlands had been bulldozed and covered, and it was subject to a million dollars in federal and local fines. Good to know!

During those months, my hopes had been rekindled, but now they were dashed again. In addition, churches, including ours, were being torn apart by political fury and fear. If we required masks to reopen, half the church felt it was too soon, and the other half accused us of caving in. Then George Floyd was killed, and the debate about race caught fire again. Some felt compassion for a downtrodden minority, but others "backed the blue"—and all of them aired their passionate feelings! We were still grieving Darrin's death as we tried to navigate these treacherous waters of anger and resentment. When we finally opened and had services again, Debbie asked me why I wasn't in my usual place in the foyer after services to greet people and shake hands with them. I told her, "That's not a safe place for me." Later, I told her, "I've been in ministry for forty years, and this is the most difficult leadership challenge I've ever experienced."

A few weeks after the Kiawah land deal fell through, one of the trustees, Brian Wells, asked to see me. He said, "Pastor, I know you're disappointed, but we haven't lost the dream. We want to help make it a reality. God will give us another piece of land, and it doesn't have to be free."

About ten days later, Brian showed me sixty-six acres near Charleston, with several buildings already on it. The setting was even better than the first property we were offered. We bought the land, and in only three months, we held our first retreat. We host fifteen pastors at a time, and as of this writing, more than 800 pastors have come through our doors. Our deep grief over losing Darrin and the added complexity and stress of trying to lead our church during the pandemic shaped the impact God has longed for us to have. We'd always had compassion for pastors, but it was heightened during this very hard season.

The pandemic and political tension has hit pastors hard. The job was difficult before, and it's become much harder. Even when Covid subsided (and I sure hope we're not in for another highly contagious variant!), it left a number of unsolved problems in its wake: many people who stopped going to church when they were closed haven't come back, and the political turmoil has continued to divide families, churches, and communities. When *Barna Group* looked at Millennials before and after the pandemic, they discovered three distinct groups:

- Holders—61% were attending the same church as before Covid shutdowns.
- Hoppers—23% are attending a different church.
- Dropouts—16% have stopped attending altogether.[2]

These stats seem to be born out in many churches. One pastor commented,

> *Our attendance is down about 20% since before Covid, but about half of those who attend now have joined since the lockdowns ended. That means only 40% of our current attenders are those who were with us before the spring of 2020. It's not quite like starting over, but it's close.*

Another recent *Barna Group* survey shows that pastoral burnout is an epidemic. When asked if they have given "real, serious consideration to quitting being in full-time ministry within the last year," 42% said "Yes." That's an almost 50% increase in only one year. Our conversations with pastors who attend our retreats shows the same measure of disillusionment. The report lists the most prevalent causes:

- Immense stress of the job—56%
- Feeling lonely and isolated—43%
- Current political divisions—38%

---

2 Barna Group, "A New Chapter in Millennial Church Attendance," August 4, 2022, https://www.barna.com/research/church-attendance-2022/.

GREG SURRATT AND CHIP JUDD

- Unhappy with the effect this role has had on my family—29%
- Not optimistic about the future of my church—29%
- Vision for the church conflicts with the church's direction—29%[3]

Can you imagine what would happen in our country if almost half of church leaders quit in one year? The ripple effect in families, churches, communities, and our nation would be catastrophic. Those who are daydreaming about quitting almost certainly aren't able to give their very best to their flocks; so even if they stay, their effectiveness is adversely affected.

Let me give a few (veiled) examples from pastors who have come to our retreats:

- "I can't trust anybody at my church. If they knew what I struggle with, I'd be out on my ear."
- "I've been the pastor at our church for just eighteen months, but the job is unsustainable. I put eighty to ninety hours a week into it, but our church isn't growing and people complain about everything . . . or so it seems. My denominational executive came to see me. I hoped he would encourage me, but before he left, he gave me a list of six things I'm doing wrong."
- "I'm thinking about going into business because business executives don't have to deal with what I do. Just

3   "Pastors Share Top Reasons They've Considered Quitting Ministry in the Past Year," Barna Group, April 27, 2022, https://www.barna.com/research/pastors-quitting-ministry/.

last week, I visited with a lady who found her husband hanging in the garage. A couple of days later, a man wept in my arms because his wife died suddenly of a heart attack. I visited a couple whose dear little boy is dying of an inoperable brain tumor. If I was a businessman, I could say, 'I'm so sorry,' and walk away. I can't do that as their pastor. I have to be there with them, suffer with them, grieve with them."

- "My two best friends and I planted our church. We were having a blast leading together, but two of us took a different perspective on politics. The one who disagreed didn't just disagree. He insisted that we agree with him, or he'd leave. He's gone now. He left a huge hole in our church and in me. My wife is devastated. She cries every day because she and my friend's wife were like sisters. Our children were best friends, and now they've taken sides. It's so tragic and unnecessary."

- "Today, people say things they never would have said years ago. Social media has given them an instant megaphone. I can't tell you how often I've read posts by people who have left our church who said really snarky things about me. One of the most common is, 'I found a church that really preaches God's Word.' But that's not the worst of it. I scroll down and read comments by people who are still at my church, and they agree with them! Years ago, people who left the church would just disappear. I wish they'd do the same thing today."

- "A guy came up to me after a service a couple of years ago and growled, 'Pastor, you're a terrible leader! You refuse to take stands on the most important issues of our day. The nation is going to hell, and you don't seem to care!' I tried to explain the theology of the kingdom of God, but he was only interested in me being a champion of his politics. The rest of the story is that his daughter was standing there listening to us. She was traumatized, and she's still in counseling two years later."

- "My heart is broken. My daughter saw the impact of the division in our church. She started cutting, and she's walked away from the faith. I pray for her every day, but she hasn't come back yet."

I could go on all day sharing stories pastors have told me. If you're one of those who is struggling—with inordinate stress, recurring temptation to sin, the wounds of "church hurt," or a combination of these—let me assure you that you aren't alone. We're in a war, not against flesh and blood, but against unseen forces (Ephesians 6:12, author paraphrase). Yes, those unseen forces animate people in our churches and our communities, but these people aren't our enemies. The world system probably isn't going to get much better (or any better) in the coming years, but Chip and I want to provide you with some effective tools to fight the right fights . . . and fight them well. The most important principle of this book, one that comforts and energizes pastors who come to our retreats, is that we're in this together. In his book, *The Four Loves*, C. S. Lewis wrote, "Friendship is born at that moment when one person says to another: 'What! You too? I thought I was the only one.'"[4]

Do you have a close friend or two, people who are genuine and caring, who don't wear a mask to hide or impress, and who don't let you wear one either? If you do, you know that these friends are treasures. If not, find at least one, and hopefully a few more. You need them.

> **The most important principle of this book, one that comforts and energizes pastors who come to our retreats, is that we're in this together.**

CHIP'S TAKE

Do you remember the movie, *The Sixth Sense*? There was a kid in the movie played by Haley Joel Osment, who had an unusual challenge. He told us about it in that famous line, "I see dead people."[5] I have a similar challenge. I see "stuck people." I see people, couples, churches, movements, nations, and the

---

4   C. S. Lewis, *The Four Loves* (New York: HarperOne, 2017).

5   Night Shyamalan, M. 1999. *The Sixth Sense*. United States: Buena Vista Pictures.

entire world stuck in cycles of thought, belief, and behavior that don't get the results they want and yet they continue day after day doing the same things but expecting a different result. Most leaders are smart, they're talented, and they've sensed God's pleasure as they entered the ministry and worked hard to build their churches, but for a variety of reasons they've hit a wall in some area of their life or leadership. They need a new set of eyes to look at themselves, their relationships, and their circumstances to break out of their self-sabotaging cycle(s) and make real progress again.

My working with leaders started with what I affectionately call "the ride." It was a pattern I saw repeated often. I began to be invited to speak occasionally at other churches because of my ability to address relational, spiritual, and emotional issues from a counseling perspective. After I was there a day or so I guess the pastor felt that he could trust me. On our way to dinner and alone in a car together the pastor would begin to share his personal struggles. I saw it happen often enough that I began to call it "the ride." After "the ride" the pastor would ask me to come back and work with his family and staff. Over time I was doing more work with the pastor, his family, and his team than I was with his church. One of the most rewarding moments for me was when I was in a meeting with several young couples on staff at a large church and one of them said to me, "You don't realize the impact you've had here, do you?" I really didn't understand what they were referring to so I asked them to elaborate. They then said, "Your meetings with the senior pastor and the rest of our leaders both individually and together has changed the culture of this church. You have brought us into a healthier place without sacrificing our capacity for growth." There is nothing they could have said that would have encouraged me more. My goal in working with leaders and their organizations, or with families, is to help them build *High Health + High-Capacity Cultures.*

A few years ago, a pastor invited me to meet with him. He'd been struggling with a range of problems for years: he wasn't happy with the performance of his team and key volunteers, and he was discouraged that his church wasn't growing as fast as he wanted. He had lived with a high level of stress, and I suppose he would have continued to live with it, but one factor caused him to change gears: he saw the effects of his long-term stress manifested in his wife's physical and emotional health. I was very impressed with his decision. My respect for him went up immediately. He was willing to make himself very uncomfortable by letting someone like me into his world for his wife's sake. Both of them, I realized, were experiencing the aging-accelerating effects of chronic stress. They were dealing with issues physically that were fairly normal about a decade beyond their current ages. Chronic stress was literally taking years off their lives. He had serious sleep problems, and he had become, well, less than pleasant to be around. In one of our first talks, he told me that he was with people all day every day, but he had no real friends.

We are all concerned about things that are happening on a national, even global scale. We're very concerned about what we see happening in the lives of our friends and fellow pastors and leaders. We, the church and those who lead it, are facing seemingly unprecedented challenges on multiple fronts. Problems are more complex and people seem less willing to work together on solving them. Greg shared the startling statistics about people in our profession from the *Barna Group* research. He and I, along with many of you, share a desire to come alongside one another and develop healthier ways to do life and ministry within the moment in which we find ourselves. It's important that we recognize that yes, some of the challenges we face are unique to our moment in history, but some of them are as old as the human race. Greg and I want to work on the things we can do to help one another *LIVE WELL and FINISH STRONG* in every area of life.

That phrase, *LIVE WELL and FINISH STRONG*, is kind of our reason for getting out of bed in the morning. If you do one you automatically do the other. If you commit yourself to living well, you will exponentially multiply the chances that you will finish strong. If you set your sights on finishing strong, it will motivate you to think, study, pray, and work at living well. We want to do both ourselves. We are also committed to helping you do the same.

Many years ago, I read a book called *Finishing Strong* by Steve Farrar. It's an excellent book. One of the thoughts that stuck with me is research they did about leaders mentioned in the Bible. Remember these numbers: 500–100–13. Farrar sites in the study that the Bible mentions 500 leaders by name and gives some details about their lives. The study also states that scripture tells us how the lives of a hundred leaders ended. The sad thing is that of those a hundred, only thirteen finished strong. Only thirteen finished having fulfilled God's purpose and while still enjoying rich fellowship with God and the people with whom they had journeyed.

> **If you commit yourself to living well, you will exponentially multiply the chances that you will finish strong.**

As I sit here writing this book, I'm sixty-nine years old and have been in ministry for forty-three years. I'm enjoying a life that is beyond what I deserve. It is not and has not been a pain-free or a mistake-free journey, but God has proven Himself faithful, kind, and relentlessly committed to both preparing a future for us and preparing us for that future. When you're at the stage of life that Greg and I are, we want you to like who you are, be pleased with what you and God have done, and enjoy deep connections with the people God has put in your life.

Whenever I get the opportunity, I find myself poking and prodding younger leaders with thoughts and questions like these.

- Think Decades: Can you live the way you're living right now for decades? If you can't, why are you living that way?
- The Trajectory Question: Can you get "there" the way you're going? Most of you have a "there" in your heart and mind. It involves your ministry dreams, hopes for your marriage and family, your finances, your health, your friendships, and your hobbies. Are you on a path that is taking you toward what you say you want? If not, what are you doing about it?
- The Insanity Question: If I keep doing what I'm doing right now the way I'm doing it right now, what will my life and my relationship with God look like in one year, in three years, in five years?

As we start this conversation together, let me tell you a few things about myself. I'm a pastor and a counselor who has spent about 13,000 hours face-to-face with wonderful people and their challenges, many of them pastors and other leaders. The pastor side of me understands the mission of the church. The counselor side of me understands, to the best of my ability, how God created us to function, what goes wrong in our growth and development, some paths to bring healing into our brokenness, and how to partner with him in bringing about progress in activating our full God-given potential. Much, if not most, of what I share in this book will come from my perspective as a metamorphologist. I'm one who has spent his life studying change:

THE ENDURANCE FACTOR

Why we need it. How it happens. Where it happens within us. Why it's harder than we make it sound. Why I think it's the most critical missing ingredient in our effort to reach the world with the life-saving power of the gospel. I pray, I think, I read, I poke and prod to learn how to create moments, environments, and experiences that bring about healing and restoration in the spirit, soul, and body of God's wonderful people.

Another important thing about me—I'm a Type 8 on the Enneagram. In case you're not into the Enneagram, let me tell you why I'm telling you that. I like to be very direct. I always want love to saturate everything I say and do. There's nothing more important to me than representing Jesus well by loving who He loves. But I'm also concerned about something I've noticed as I've worked with individuals, leaders, and their organizations. There's not enough truth-telling going on. I don't mean everyone's lying, although that's happening some. I mean there's not enough people around who have the conviction of having the hard conversations when they need to happen. Here's how I see it.

In John 8:31-32 Jesus says, "If you continue in my word, then you are truly My disciples, and you will know the truth, and the truth will set you free." In light of what I said earlier about myself, that I see "stuck people," here's another way to represent the message of that passage. "You shall know the truth, and the truth that you come to know will get you "unstuck."

When you find yourself stuck in an area of your life, pay attention. It might be in the area of relationships. It could be a challenge in your management of your emotions, or some troubling behavior pattern that continues to pull you in directions that are destructive for you and hurtful to others. Maybe you have tried, possibly for years, to break out of that cycle on your own. I've found that staying stuck is always the absence of, insufficiency of, or misapplication of truth.

When you find yourself in your personal life repeating a cycle, there is truth available to break you out of that cycle. When you find yourself in your professional life, pastoring your church, or dealing with a repeating pattern that is frustrating and debilitating, there is truth available to set you free from that cycle. I believe most of us live without the level of truth we need to gain insight into our true condition. Somehow, we've equated being truthful with being unkind. God showed me years ago that it is just as unloving to have grace without truth, as it is to speak truth without grace.

By the way, the higher you go on the organizational chart, the less truth you get.

> God showed me years ago that it is just as unloving to have grace without truth, as it is to speak truth without grace.

THE ENDURANCE FACTOR

Pastors hire me to come into their awesome churches to get what I call "behind the curtain" insight into the culture and reality of how things really work around there. They usually bring me in because they're stuck in some area. There's some dimension of ministry that they feel they need help with. My commitment to them is that I will prayerfully speak the truth as honestly and directly as I can. If I'm insecure, afraid, or unable to see and say what I believe will help them break out of their stuckness, then I'm not doing my job and I'm unable to help them and their teams.

This is a really important thought for every leader to consider. Most leaders don't have loving, trusted sources of direct and honest feedback. I've observed that the higher you go on the organizational chart, the less truth you get. When I'm working with a pastor and we're talking about his situation, he'll often tell me that his team can say anything they want to him. He's confident that he has several people around him that would correct him and challenge him when he needs it. I have found it is almost never true. Think about it for a minute. Most of them love their leader, trust their leader, and are there to serve that leader, and help him fulfill the assignment that's on his/her life. Also, they need that leader's approval, recognition, and love, on top of the fact that he signs their paycheck. It's not automatic or natural to create an environment where truth runs uphill.

Almost fifteen years ago, Mac Lake was on the staff at Seacoast, where Greg was the lead pastor, and he brought me in to work with the team. After my second meeting with them,

Greg asked me to step into his office. I was the pastor of a little church about forty miles north of Charleston; Greg was kind of a big deal (at least he thought so)—and I was more than a bit intimidated. As we talked, he explained that he felt stuck. He was waking up every morning without the fire he'd felt and the vision he'd lived with for so long. He said, "I feel dishonest because I'm taking a salary, and I don't burn with the same passion I once did for growing Seacoast Church."

The day before, I sensed God give me a word for Greg, but I had no idea if, when, or how I would deliver it. Now was the time. I said, "I believe God gave me a word for you. Can I share it with you?"

He nodded and said, "Yes."

I shared what I felt God had impressed on my heart:

Greg, you can't build tomorrow's church, but you can build the leaders who will build tomorrow's church. Tomorrow's church is not for you, so God's not going to give you a vision for it. He's going to give the vision to the young leaders who will be around to build it. Your job is to prepare them.

He stared at me for a little while, and then he said, "Okay. I get it."

That moment was the beginning of our relationship, a bond of trust and respect that I will always treasure. It didn't take me long to observe that Greg is the same person everywhere he goes: on stage and in the car, leading a team or having dinner, talking about the Lord, and talking about sports. A particular scene that really impressed me was when he and I were walking to a meeting. We had a schedule to keep, but he stopped to talk to a janitor with some mental challenges who was picking up trash in the offices. Greg treated him the same way he'd treat a king, a president, his father, a friend, you, me, or anyone else he values. He never talks down to anyone because he doesn't believe he's above anyone. As I watched this interaction, I thought, *This is a guy I could follow.*

After a couple of years consulting with Seacoast Church and a number of other churches, I went through a succession process at the church where I was a pastor. God brought us a great guy to replace me, and suddenly I was free as a bird. I loved it! However, one day I sensed God ask me, "Are you willing to give up your freedom?" About two months later, Greg asked me to pray about coming on the staff at Seacoast. I burst out in tears because I knew it was a fulfillment of God's challenge to my wife and me. God was challenging us to step into a larger sphere of responsibility and influence than we had ever experienced before. We were honored beyond words.

I get church growth. I really do. I understand the drive to reach more people, disciple more people, and send more people into the harvest. But I'm not focused on the mechanics of building a church; I'm focused on the mechanics of building a life. I tell leaders, "The greatest barriers between you and the future you want are inside you, not outside. The only person who can take you out of the will of God is you, not anyone else." The seeds of our challenges today—with our own sin, our marriages, our kids, our teams, and our people—were sown many years ago when we were children. If we don't understand that, and if we don't find a way to address those long-buried presuppositions about ourselves, God, and others, we'll ask the wrong questions and come up with ineffective answers. My part of this book is aimed at asking the right questions so you can find the right answers.

I've said all of this to highlight two things. The first is that I like to be truthful and direct. So, you've been warned. The second is to challenge you with this question: What sources of truthfulness do you have in your life and ministry? Are you a truth chaser or a truth avoider? As we go forward discussing some of the topics to come, I trust you will get a clearer and clearer sense of which of those two you are.

The greatest barriers between you and the future you want are inside you, not outside. The only person who can take you out of the will of God is you, not anyone else.

CHAPTER 2

WE'RE ALL FROGS

GREG'S TAKE

I got fired from my first three jobs in ministry. When I was in college, my dad hired me to be the youth pastor at his church, which was about sixty miles from where I was going to school. My little Honda got fifty miles to the gallon, and gas was only about forty cents a gallon, so I drove back and forth every weekend. My dad paid me five dollars a week. One Saturday night, I took a couple of the girls in the youth group to a movie—*Towering Inferno*. Someone who went to the church was there and saw me, and he ratted me out to my dad before church the next morning. When the service was over, Dad called me into his office. He asked, "Son, did you go to a movie?"

"Yes, sir, I did."

"Did you take some girls?"

"Yes, sir. I did that too."

Dad told me in no uncertain terms, "Greg, you can go to hell if you want to, but you're not going to corrupt the morals of girls in our church. You're fired." That was number one.

After graduation, my grandfather asked me to join him in California as the youth pastor at his church in Santa Monica. He neglected to tell me that the church was in the middle of an acrimonious split. He hoped my presence would somehow change the atmosphere. It didn't, and about two months after I arrived, it all blew up. During the service, people got up and yelled nasty accusations at each other. A man sitting next to me got up and said some very ugly things. I was a wrestler in high school, and I was just about to put a hammer lock on him and throw him to the ground. Thankfully, I didn't do that or I might have been arrested. My grandfather called the District Superintendent to come for a church business meeting, and at the meeting, both of us were fired. The church gave each of us $500 as a severance, which made me feel like a millionaire. I got a flight back to Colorado. That's firing number two; but in that case, it wasn't really my fault. The experience made a big impact on me, and I avoided church for a while.

I went to work for Hewlett-Packard, married Debbie, and settled into a fairly comfortable life. In fact, the company offered me a very substantial raise and bonuses to participate in opening a new plant in Corvallis, Oregon. At that point, Debbie and I were living large. Before we left, we had started attending a little Assemblies of God church. The pastor asked me to have breakfast with him one morning, and he asked me to join his staff team. He offered me $6,500 . . . a year, not a month. He wanted Debbie to join the team, too. We sensed this was what God wanted us to do, so we traded our new sports car for an old beater, and we moved out of our nice apartment into government housing. I had no idea what I was getting into. The church was building a new facility, and the pastor was the general contractor. He put me to work in construction Monday through Friday and half a day on Saturday. He told me that Sunday was my day off, but I led worship in the morning service, the youth group in the afternoon, and worship again for the evening service—so much for a day off. After a year, he fired me. He told me, "You need to go back to Hewlett-Packard because you're never going to make it in ministry." I wanted to say, "But this isn't ministry. It's construction," but I didn't say that. That's number three.

Debbie and I loaded up a little trailer and drove to St. Louis where we moved into my parents' basement. Debbie bought a used book for twenty-five cents called, *All Originality Makes a Dull Church* by Dan Baumann[6], which basically called pastors to learn from the original ideas of others. My uncle was a district official in Illinois, and he asked me if I wanted to be a candidate for a church of nine people. I responded with an

---

6   Dan Baumann, *All Originality Makes a Dull Church* (Santa Ana, CA: Vision House Publishers, 1976).

enthusiastic, "Yes!" Debbie and I drove to the little town with our newborn in tow. I was scheduled to teach Sunday school, preach on Sunday morning, and speak again on Sunday night before the vote. After the morning service, they told me not to bother coming back that night. They weren't interested in me being their pastor.

I was discouraged, but Debbie was relieved. When I told my uncle what had happened, he said, "That's okay. I have another church where you can try out. It's substantially bigger—thirteen people." The next Sunday, we drove to Freeport, Illinois. I preached my only three prepared sermons on Sunday morning, Sunday night, and Wednesday night. I got eleven votes, so I was the new pastor. But I had a problem: after those three messages, my folder was bare.

I had to come up with content for three messages for the next week, and I scrambled to find something to say. A few weeks into this role, the "blizzard of '79" hit the Midwest. Feet of snow blanketed the area, and the temperature didn't rise above freezing for months. The stress of the job and the dismal weather got to me. For the first time in my life, I was depressed . . . so depressed that I didn't get out of bed each day unless I absolutely had to. For six months, my Dad sent me the notes for his sermons. I'm sure his messages were really good, but mine were horrible. I was at the end. We drove down to see my parents, and on the way, I told Debbie, "I can't do this. Obviously, I misunderstood God's call. Let's turn on I-70 and go to Colorado.

I can get my old job at Hewlett-Packard." Debbie and my Dad encouraged me to keep going. I didn't want to, but I did.

At about that time, I found a book, *Telling Yourself the Truth*, by William Backus. The principles I learned about replacing negative thoughts with positive ones saved my ministry. Later, I learned the book is based on cognitive-behavioral therapy, which correlates very well with biblical models of life change.

In 1988, we launched Seacoast, and on that first Sunday, on Easter, we had 340 people. I was so excited. I called a friend in Denver and said, "You'd better get down here and help me! God is doing something amazing at our church plant! A revival is breaking out!" Nobody told me that a lot of people who attend on the first Sunday don't come back for the second one. Yes, we had a revival, but it was "a Gideon revival"—for three years, our attendance declined.

My excitement after the launch date quickly devolved into deep discouragement. I went to the elders of the church that sponsored our plant and told them, "Let's end it right here. This was a swing and a miss." I tried to convince them three times to let me resign, but each time they encouraged me to hang in there.

It took five years for our average attendance to go back to what we had on that first Sunday. When we finally got some momentum, no one was more surprised than me. I call Seacoast "the slowest growing megachurch in the history of the world." Our story has been a comfort for a lot of church planters who had dreams of rapid growth and were disappointed when it didn't happen like they hoped.

THE ENDURANCE FACTOR

When a friend heard me tell the saga of being fired three times, being depressed during a blizzard, and planting a church that refused to grow for years, he asked, "What did you learn from all that?"

"Good question," I answered. "First, I'd say that anything I learned isn't past tense. I'm still learning that it's important to tell myself the right story. For instance, when someone left our church, for years I took it as personal rejection, but I've been learning to tell myself a different story: Maybe it's not personal at all, maybe the Lord led them to harvest in another field, or maybe they had a change of career or family situation. I'm a first-class catastrophizer. If something is a little bad, I can blow it up into a monumental disaster. I imagine the worst, I think of all the horrible things people are probably saying about me, and I don't see any hopeful outcome. That's why I desperately need to change the story.

Three important factors are important in my story: identity, calling, and assignment. The first one, my *identity*, rests on the foundation of God's grace, love, and strength. God created Adam and Eve in His image; they were "image bearers," and so am I. The writer to the Hebrews tells us that Jesus was the accurate reflection of God's image, but you and I have the privilege of representing Him to everyone around us. How did this happen? It's only and always based on the grace of God. We were hopelessly lost and deserving of eternal punishment for our sins, but Jesus took our place to do for us what we couldn't do for ourselves. In Paul's letters, he uses a particular shorthand to describe the elements of our identity. He says we're "in Christ" or "in Him." We're "in Him" in His death, so all of our sins are completely forgiven; we're "in Him" in His resurrection, so we have new life and a new connection with God; we're "in Him" in His life, so the righteousness of Jesus has been credited to our account; and we're "in Him" in the ascension, so we're seated with Christ at the right hand of the Father. Those are legal, forensic truths that amaze us, but God goes to great lengths to convince us that the legal facts in the courtroom are only the beginning of a rich, vibrant, intimate relationship with Him. For instance, in Exodus 19 and 1 Peter 2, we're called "a special possession," a term that means "treasure." God considers you and me to be His treasure! In Paul's prayer in Ephesians 1, he writes, "I pray that the eyes of your heart may be enlightened, so that you will know what is the hope of His calling, what are the riches of the glory of His inheritance in the saints, and what is the boundless greatness of His power toward us who believe . . ." (Ephesians 1:18-19). "Know" is more than head knowledge (*gnosis*); it's *epignosis,* or heart-felt experience. He wants his readers to feel the warmth of their identity which he described in the first verses of the chapter, the hope of our calling: we're chosen, loved, forgiven, and sealed by the Holy Spirit. He wants us to feel the wonder that God considers Himself to be rich because He has us, and He wants us to live in the fullness of the Holy Spirit's presence and power. Sometimes, as we all know too well, we don't feel God's warmth and presence. When His people complained that He had forgotten them, God assured them: "Can a woman forget her nursing child, And not have compassion on the son of her womb? Surely, they may forget, Yet I will not forget you. Behold, I have inscribed you on the palms of My hands . . ." (Isaiah 49:15-16).

> ## The hope of our calling: we're chosen, loved, forgiven, and sealed by the Holy Spirit.

Justification is the bedrock of our faith, but the doctrine of adoption carries us to the heart of God. Author and professor J. I. Packer explains, "Adoption is the highest privilege that the gospel offers: higher even than justification. . . . to be right with God the Judge is a great thing, but to be loved and cared for by God the Father is greater."[7]

Now, I'm not trying to insult you by writing at some length about the power and wonder of the gospel of grace. You know these things: you preach them and teach them all the time. The problem is that it's easy to gnosis them without epignosis of them. It's like the difference between audio and video. When we listen to music or a podcast, it's easy for our minds to wander,

---

7 J. I. Packer and Carolyn Nystrom, *Knowing God Devotional Journal: A One-Year Guide* (Carol Stream, IL: InterVarsity Press, 2009), p.231.

but when we're looking at a video, the images on the screen capture us more completely. Far too often, God's grace is on audio for us, and performance, metrics, and reputations are on video. That needs to change.

How often do we need to reorient our focus on the video of grace? As often as it takes. The encouragement to "remember" is scattered throughout the Scriptures. Why? Because it's so easy to forget. When we take communion, Paul tells us to remember the broken body and shed blood of Jesus: "For as often as you eat this bread and drink the cup, you proclaim the Lord's death until He comes" (1 Corinthians 11:26). One ancient tradition says that "as often as you eat this bread and drink the cup" refers to every meal, not just communion. What would it mean to us if we intentionally reminded ourselves and each other of Christ's sacrifice far more often? We'd be more regularly amazed that we were helpless and hopeless apart from Christ's saving grace, but now we're more valuable to Him than all the stars in the skies and all the jewels, gold, and silver found in the earth. And what does being immersed in grace do to us, for us, and in us? Paul explained, "Christ's love controls us. Since we believe that Christ died for all, we also believe that we have all died to our old life. He died for everyone so that those who receive his new life will no longer live for themselves. Instead, they will live for Christ, who died and was raised for them" (2 Corinthians 5:14-15, NLT). When we're blown away by grace, Christ's love propels, directs, and energizes everything we say and do.

THE ENDURANCE FACTOR

My *calling* is the same as Adam and Eve's—to bring the kingdom rule of God to every place on earth. As Jesus taught us to pray, "Your kingdom come, Your will be done" (Matthew 6:10). What are the characteristics of God's kingdom? The fruit of the Spirit, yes, caring for the poor, certainly, and putting kindness, righteousness, and justice in the forefront of every thought, word, and action. In his letter to the Ephesians, Paul painted this picture of a person committed to deepening and extending God's kingdom: "Therefore I, the prisoner of the Lord, urge you to walk in a manner worthy of the calling with which you have been called, with all humility and gentleness, with patience, bearing with one another in love, being diligent to keep the unity of the Spirit in the bond of peace" (Ephesians 4:1-3).

How can we know we're in the right calling? I think about the scene in *Chariots of Fire* when Eric Liddell was training for the 1924 Olympics. His sister Jenny was sure that Eric's true calling was to be a missionary, and he should give up the frivolous pursuit (in her estimation) of representing Scotland in the Olympics. Eric turned to her and said, "Jenny, Jenny. God made me fast, and when I run, I feel His pleasure."[8] When do you and I feel God's pleasure? When is there a strong sense that we're in the sweet spot, doing what God has crafted us to do? That, perhaps as much as any other measurement or description, lets us know we're following God's call.

The first two factors, identity and calling, are constants; they never change. But my *assignment* may be different from one

---

8   Hugh Hudson. 1981. *Chariots of Fire*. United States: 20th Century Fox.

period of my life to another (and if I'm fired, the period may not last long!). I've had *macro*-assignments as a husband, father, being a youth pastor, working at Hewlett-Packard, leading a small church at Seacoast, as the founder of a church-planting movement, and now in a ministry to care for pastors. But I've also had *micro*-assignments to live out my identity as God's beloved child and my calling to help establish the kingdom rule of God by being kind to the barista at the coffee shop, stopping to help someone who dropped her groceries, and any of a zillion other moments that I represent the King of kings to the people whose path I cross each day. In all of these, my identity hasn't budged an inch, and my calling has been consistent. I can be God's beloved child and live for the kingdom wherever I go, whoever I'm with, and however God leads me.

A number of people have asked, "Greg, how do you feel now that you're not the lead pastor at Seacoast? You were a big deal then."

I always reply, "I feel great!" That role was, in fact, wonderful, but leaving it didn't affect my identity or my calling in the least. It only changed my assignment. Over the years, I had to learn that my identity didn't center around my assignment. If and when it did, I became fixated on my performance, the metrics of the church, and what others were saying about me. That's not a stable place to be!

When pastors have their identity and calling right, they still have plenty of problems to overcome, but they rest on the bedrock of God's love and purpose for them. When their sense of who they are, their value, and their reputation come from externals—success and fame—they're always looking over their shoulders, always worried about risks or taking huge risks, and always checking out their social media accounts to see what people are saying about them. Their consuming goal becomes image management . . . it's all about them, so people are valuable if they contribute positively to that image, and they're threats if they don't.

Comparison kills. Chip isn't affected much by people's opinions, but I am. I've had to fight all my life to retell my story so it's all about Jesus and not all about me. That's why I had to think, study, and pray to come up with clarity about the three factors. With these insights, I could rest in my identity and calling and give everything I've got to my God-given assignment, knowing that He defines success, not me or the people who are watching me. Far too often, we're not being fair when we compare ourselves to "more successful" pastors. We look at their glowing social media posts, and all we can think about is our "Not Top Ten."

I've been learning to limit my sense of burden to those things that I'm truly responsible for. I pastored in a small-town community that lost a large percentage of their population over a relatively short period of time. That demographic loss was completely outside my control. I was still responsible to invest my heart in my assignment, but with this insight, my expectations were more in line with reality. But I've also pastored in a community, Mt. Pleasant, that has ballooned in size, bringing many more people in contact with the people of our church. Was I responsible for the growth of our city? Not in the least, so I can't take credit for much of our church's growth.

In Chip's part of this chapter, he'll talk about the normalization of stress, so that we don't even notice as it increases. That's what he means by the title of this chapter, referring to "the frog in the kettle." My angle on the title is different: Like the princess that kisses the frog that turns into a prince, you and I are frogs who have been kissed by the grace of God in Jesus, and it turns us into dearly beloved children of God.

CHIP'S TAKE

There I was, curled up in a ball in the fetal position, crying uncontrollably. I was lying on my bed, my wife was sitting with me, and one of my best friends, Phillip Miles, a pastor I've known for decades, was on the phone attempting to make sense of this moment. I was known as someone who was emotionally strong and stable, and no one would have ever expected to see me this way. I kind of knew what was happening, but I couldn't seem to do anything about it. It ambushed me from out of nowhere. I felt helpless, afraid, irrational, embarrassed, ashamed, and trapped, feeling like it would never end. I didn't want anyone to see me this way.

These are the symptoms I was experiencing:

- A sense of impending doom, that something horrible is about to happen.
- A strong, irrational feeling of fear and foreboding.

- A Sense of confusion.
- Extreme emotional distress. Panicky feelings.
- Racing fearful thoughts.
- An inability to calm myself down.
- Tingling sensations in my chest and down my arms.

It was a Thursday afternoon. I had just finished what we call a "message run-through" at Seacoast Church. What that means is the person speaking on the following weekend does an actual, full run-through of their message on Thursday afternoon. We all do it. I had done it several times before this. The purpose is to get feedback and clarification on how well the message is flowing and landing on the people listening. The challenge is that you're on stage in a room that seats 2,400 people and there's only about ten or twelve people sitting there. They're spread around the room, looking at their phones, and giving very little tangible encouragement. We affectionately call it waterboarding. It is a great practice, and has helped all of us as communicators, but it's not a fun experience even on a good day. This was not a good day. I was about halfway through my message and I realized it wasn't working. I felt disconnected from my audience, all twelve of them. I could tell I had too much information and I was going into too much detail. I knew the message was not going to work, but I had to finish it so I could get helpful feedback and judge the timing. Not a fun moment, but at the same time, not life-shattering either. So I never expected what was going to happen several hours after that. Here's an interesting side-note—my title was *Chasing*

Sunshine. The message was about managing your emotions. I called my wife to tell her I wouldn't be home right away. I told her the "message run-through" hadn't gone well and I was going to stay and work on my message. I was a little frustrated, but I felt normal. When I arrived home, the bottom fell out. It was as if I had a global, systemwide crash of my mental and emotional stability. It was awful.

We didn't have the teaching team we do now. Pastor Greg and Pastor Josh were out of town. I didn't feel like I had any options. All I could envision was having to hit the panic button and rearranging the weekend because of my emotional breakdown. Oh, by the way, I'm the staff counselor. I'm the guy who studies and teaches on mental and emotional health at Seacoast and around the country. As you can imagine, my mind was imploding with all of the implications if I had to cancel my speaking on the weekend at the last minute. In hindsight, I know that Pastor Greg and Pastor Josh would have handled it with grace and understanding. But in the moment, in the condition I was in, that wasn't how I saw it playing out.

I did speak that weekend, and it went very well. God helped me in ways I'll describe shortly, but I also received help from a medical doctor who understood what I was experiencing from a physiological perspective. Let's go there first. My first response was to tough it out and trust God to get me through it quickly. Within several hours my confidence in that scenario was weakened, particularly with my need to rework my message and be ready to speak in forty-eight hours. The doctor prescribed two medications: one to treat the symptoms, and the other to treat the physiological cause. The first one brings immediate relief, and the other takes weeks to have a tangible effect. I'm sharing the part the medication played because I know that many of you are currently on medication, may need to be at some point in the future, or need to understand the blessing meds can be when a problem is clearly physiological in nature.

God helped by giving insight into how I got there and by putting me in a place to connect with my own emotions and the emotions of the people who would hear the message and needed the grace and truth that it brought. Let me share a few thoughts that I felt led to put in the message.

"Was it a coincidence that it happened the very week that I was to speak on managing your emotions?"

I don't think so. I don't believe God caused my situation, but I believe He chose to use it. The truth is, I was going to address this topic from a place of safe and consistent victory. I was doing extremely well—traveling and speaking, ministering to other churches, and coming home to this awesome church. I was riding high and running hard. I was going to give information and insights from studies and counseling experience. But it would not have come with the emotional connection and compassion that I have had in the past.

"So, what did I get out of this patch of unpleasant, stormy weather? Here are several observations that God helped me make, as I was beginning to feel like myself again."

- I have some unprocessed, toxic emotions connected to some situations I was pretending didn't bother me.
- I was avoiding things that bothered me through various forms of escape.
- I wasn't listening to my emotions and allowing them to lead me toward health and freedom.
- I wasn't being honest with myself and with God about some disappointments over the years and how they affected my trust in Him, and therefore, my sense of feeling safe and secure in this world.
- I wasn't slowing down to allow God to talk to me at a deeper level and help me make adjustments that need to be made.
- I wasn't honoring the way He created me to live by being a good steward of my life rhythms and energy.

"This is a really important point: No one did this to me! I did!"

I don't believe God caused my situation, but I believe He chose to use it.

THE ENDURANCE FACTOR

Let me say to you, the reader of this book, what I said to them that weekend: There are two reasons I am sharing my experience with you today:

First, there are individuals, pastors, and leaders reading these words who are being affected by issues and emotions, and they need to know we're here for them, and more importantly, that God hasn't forgotten them and He's here for them. They're carrying burdens and enduring struggles that involve children, parents, finances, health, and ministry challenges that drain their emotional and spiritual resources. They often feel isolated, helpless, and ashamed. I want to make sure they know they're not isolated, they're not helpless, and they have no need to feel ashamed.

And second: The truth will set us free. There are things we can learn, experience, and practice that will break destructive cycles and help us find and follow the narrow path that leads to life.

In that message, about ten years ago, I shared what I called "Tools for Chasing Sunshine." I shared four things that we could learn and practice that would break destructive cycles and build soul-nourishing rhythms into our lives. These four "tools" have become the pillars that can help you *LIVE WELL and FINISH STRONG*. Here they are as I presented them ten years ago.

1) "Own your emotions."
2) "Don't let the ANTs ruin your picnic. (ANTs are Automatic Negative Thoughts.)
3) "Slow down regularly and quiet yourself on the inside and the outside.
4) "Build a loving support system and get the help you need."

As the dust settled and the weekend was over, God had done some awesome work. The message received a spontaneous standing ovation. Why? Because people felt understood and loved in the midst of their struggles. They sensed that we as pastors and leaders deal with the same challenges they do. And they were right. That's why Greg and I are writing this book. We want to create safe places for pastors and leaders to get real and find the help they need in non-judgmental environments. Real freedom awaits us if we're willing to take off our masks and experience the depth of relationship and community that God designed us for.

> **Real freedom awaits us if we're willing to take off our masks and experience the depth of relationship and community that God designed us for.**

Now let's talk about what I learned as a result of "my crash," which is what I affectionately call that moment in my life. Forgive me for my arrogance and presumption, but I believe this will really help some of you. I believe anxiety has become an epidemic in our culture and unfortunately, within the church and its leaders. I also believe that when we understand how stress—particularly chronic stress—affects us, it will release us from shame and empower us to build rituals and rhythms that both heal and protect us from the disruptive effects of chronic stress.

So, what happened? How did I get there? I had studied anxiety, panic attacks, and the effects of stress, but I never thought I would experience it from the inside out. If you knew me fifteen years ago, you would never have thought that I would deal with anxiety or have a crash like I did. I only have two gears: on and off. When I'm on, I'm really on. When I'm off, I'm really off. I'm either engaged intensely in some project or I'm engaged intensely in some form of escape or fun.

The few years before coming on staff at Seacoast were everything I've ever dreamed of. My wife Coleen and I had transitioned the leadership of our church to a great couple. We were traveling and speaking, coaching, and consulting churches several times a month. We had a great group of friends and relationships in which we felt loved and respected. We lived in a condo, with a golf course out the back door and a pool out the front. Coleen and I had developed and practiced a very soul-nourishing rhythm in our spiritual lives that included Bible reading and study, prayer, journaling, and consistent connection with a group of other pastors who encouraged and challenged us in really healthy ways. When we weren't traveling, we could read, pray, study, or just sit out at our pool and get refreshed by God's awesome love. As I shared in chapter one, we sensed God was asking us to give up our freedom for the next season.

This is when Pastor Greg asked us to pray about coming onto the staff at Seacoast Church. We were honored beyond words and felt God leading us clearly in that direction. We were hired with the understanding that I could continue to do what I was doing ministering to other churches and their leaders.

There was nothing about Seacoast that contributed to my crash. The pathway toward the crash was trickier than that. Before coming on staff at Seacoast, I regularly went through what I called "travel gauntlets," several weeks where I barely had time to think. I would go to several churches, be home for a few days, then hit the road again. But when each gauntlet was over, I could unplug, refresh, and recharge sitting with my awesome wife out by our condo pool. After coming on staff at Seacoast, I was in a new environment with new responsibilities, expectations, and opportunities. I still traveled a few times a month but with a very important difference. Now when I came home, I couldn't just sit by the pool and chill. I was coming home to an awesome mega-church with unlimited needs for what I loved to do. No one at Seacoast made me feel pressured or judged, but I wanted them to be glad they had chosen me to be a part of their team.

Most of what I'm about to say I learned as a result of my crash. It has been really helpful to me and to many of the leaders with whom I've worked over the last ten years since then. I hope it will make as much sense to you as it has to me, and that it will be helpful in both recovering from and preventing stress-related challenges in your life.

THE ADRENALINE CYCLE

Understanding the adrenaline cycle and its effects has been key in my recovery and the maintenance of healthier rhythms and the rituals (consistently practiced, life-giving habits) that support those rhythms. My thoughts here will be a generalized, summarized explanation with as little complicated biology and science as necessary. We will discuss the interaction between two hormones, adrenaline and serotonin, even though there are more involved.

Adrenaline is a hormone released by the central nervous system in response to stress, anger, or fear. It has mental and emotional effects, as well as physiological effects. It enhances our ability to deal with real or perceived threats and challenges. It's very important to understand that your adrenaline cycle is triggered by either positive or negative stress. Your brain is incapable of telling the difference. When you are in an excited state dealing with a threat or challenge, your brain's chemical response is the same as it is when you're in an excited state of enjoyment or arousal.

God designed us to be energized and equipped by adrenaline as we rise up to deal with temporary challenges. We feel alert, strong, focused, and confident. We like the feeling. It carries a sense of empowerment. However, God never intended us to live under its influence for prolonged periods of time. He designed us to recover from its effects by "flushing" it out of our system through intentional, deep rest and recovery. When we don't consistently do that, we experience the negative effects of adrenaline. Unflushed adrenaline resulting from chronic arousal and stress is corrosive to our system. According to the late Dr. Archibald Hart, "When stress is chronic—that is when it is continuous and doesn't let up or allow the body adequate time to recover, the following happens:

1) "The immune system becomes depleted. We get sick more often. We don't heal as fast. There is strong evidence that we're more vulnerable to certain diseases.

2) "The anti-pain system becomes depleted. Your body has pain-killing hormones, such as endorphins, that control pain during stress. When the demands are unrelenting the endorphins become depleted. The result is an increased sensitivity to pain and a lowered tolerance for discomfort.

3) "The anti-anxiety system becomes depleted. Like endorphins for physical pain, the body has tranquilizers to inhibit anxiety. Under prolonged conditions of stress, these tranquilizers become depleted and the emotional experience of stress goes up. We become prone to more anxious mental and emotional states."[9]

The other critical effect of chronic stress that leads us to hyperadrenalism is the decrease of our serotonin levels. Serotonin is the "feel-good hormone." It decreases anxiety and physiological stress and improves our mood. It helps us to feel happy, safe, and content. When our serotonin levels are decreased, we are susceptible to both anxiety and depression. I found that the

---

9   Archibald Hart, *Adrenaline and Stress: The Exciting New Breakthrough That Helps You Overcome Stress* Damage (Nashville: Thomas Nelson, 1995), Part 1.

ingredients for my crash are explained within those last paragraphs. As I share what I learned about myself, see what parts apply to you and your life rhythms.

I had become an adrenaline addict. I had lived in a state of chronic arousal for so long, somewhere between three to five years, that being under the influence of adrenaline felt normal to me. I felt like superman. I had more energy, more focus, more stamina. Enjoyment of the effect made me blind to the unintended consequences. I was more selfish and short-tempered. I was rarely fully present with anyone. Anything that didn't move me in the direction of my immediate objective was seen as an irritant. My intimacy with God became transactional. My journal that had always been the center of my conversational relationship with God was virtually empty. When I would take time off, it would take days for me to unwind and feel rested and calm.

My crash wasn't caused by specific things that produced stress. It was caused by the depletion of serotonin in my brain due to long stretches of chronic, unflushed adrenaline as a result of my unchecked engagement with a life filled with things I loved to do. Remember, the brain doesn't distinguish between good and bad stress. It's chemical response is the same for both. The crash was literally *the result of too much of a good thing.* I had drifted away from the spiritual rituals and rhythms that had been so life-giving to me. I had over-taxed my emotional threat-detection center to the point that it was stuck on the ON setting. Everything felt like a threat—even fun things that created a state of excitement. I had jacked-up my brain's ability to manage anxiety and the everyday challenges of life. In a nutshell, this is what I'm trying to communicate:

CHRONIC STRESS (Positive or Negative)
leads to
ADRENALINE ADDICTION
which leads to
LOW SEROTONIN
which leads to
ANXIETY & DEPRESSION

I was helped by God, a great wife, good friends, the return to life-giving spiritual rhythms, and some well-managed medical attention from a skilled physician. It took time to get back to being myself. I stayed on medication for a couple of years, and I returned to the spiritual rhythms that had served me so well in the past. We will talk specifically about them later in the book.

Please give serious thought and reflection to these issues. Meet regularly with some trusted friends who have proven they love you and will speak truth to you when it's difficult. Remember—we're all frogs.

CHAPTER 3

A PRICE TOO HIGH

GREG'S TAKE

A few years ago at a conference, Dr. Richard Swenson, the author of *Margin: Restoring Emotional, Physical, Financial, and Time Reserves to Overloaded Lives*,[10] explained the cumulative impact of stress. He told the audience to look outside the window and look at a tree. If someone bent a branch a little bit, when it was released, it would quickly go back to its original, relaxed position. If the person bent it much more, it might stay bent. And if he bent it so far that it broke, it was almost impossible to restore the branch to the original shape.

---

10 Richard A. Swenson, *Margin: Restoring Emotional, Physical, Financial, and Time Reserves to Overloaded Lives* (Colorado Springs, CO: NavPress).

THE ENDURANCE FACTOR

He explained that this was a picture of what stress does in the human body. If we're not careful, we might become irreparably broken—we can mend to a certain extent, but we won't ever be what we were before. The audience gasped at the thought that a person might pass the point of no return, but Dr. Swenson had seen enough patients to know the truth. It's too high a price to pay for one more day of pushing, one more sleepless night of worry, and one more moment when we pressure people instead of loving them.

We put enormous emphasis on church metrics. Yes, shepherds need to know the condition of their flocks, but far too often, numbers (or the lack of numbers) are our primary driver. . . . and it's a cruel master. We all know stories of leaders who were so fixated on growing their churches that they sacrificed everything—family, reputation, health, and honor—for their churches to grow. But we don't hear the stories of so many who are caught up in this rat race but never make the news. They pay a high price too. Of course, some who are driven give up or collapse; they become passive, but not out of choice.

An organization's culture is a reflection of its leader. No one else has the power and the microphone the leader possesses. In the church, pastors who are driven by metrics without a foundation of grace use people instead of loving them and helping them live out of their identity and calling. These team members are deeply affected: they either replicate the leader's loveless drive, or they try to form a resistance movement within the team. Sadly, most of these leaders insist their team is a family, but it's a dysfunctional one that confuses people. Staff members want to believe the leader is a good, noble, loving person because it makes them feel safe (and it's terrifying to think of saying the leader isn't), so some keep believing it even in the face of contrary evidence, but others bail out because it's so unhealthy. Some assume their culture is just like every other church, so they just buckle down and bear it, but others know better. They may try to change the culture from a subordinate position, which puts them at odds with the pastor who accuses them of not being team players.

> **An organization's culture is a reflection of its leader. No one else has the power and the microphone the leader possesses.**

I wasn't immune to the lure of impressive metrics. When our church started growing really fast in the late 90s, I lost perspective. My normal rhythms of adrenaline and rest were short-circuited, and I lived on adrenaline virtually all the time. As we grew, we needed to add services, and I was sure I needed to speak at the vast majority of them. One Easter, we scheduled eight services, and I was speaking at all of them. Each spring, my allergies cause a world of problems. When I was tested, I was allergic to thirty-one out of the thirty-two allergens. I came back to the church to show my team the welts on my arm where the test had been performed. It was lit up like a Christmas tree! Very impressive! On this particular weekend, I had my normal spring sinus infection. I felt lousy, and I had trouble stanching the flow of snot. (Sorry for the visual, but it's part of the story.) After the sixth service, I was so spent that I went in our green room and laid down on the sofa. In minutes, a pile of snot-filled tissues were on the floor next to me. One of our assistant pastors, Shawn Wood, walked in and saw my condition. He asked, "Pastor, do you have two more in you?"

I just told him, "Look at me. What do you think?"

Sean said, "No problem. I'll get you fixed up." He went next door to a pharmacy and bought a couple of Red Bulls, a bottle of antihistamine, and a six-pack of Mountain Dew. When he walked back in, he said, "Pastor, swallow this antihistamine and down it with a Red Bull, and then chase it with Mountain Dew." I was desperate, so I did what I was told.

Oh man, it worked! I don't know if I've ever been as up for a message as those last two. The moral of the story is obvious: you can either trust the Holy Spirit to empower you to speak, or you can drink some Red Bull, take a pill, down a bottle of Mountain Dew, and let it fly!

Yes, I'm trying to get a smile out of that story, but the truth is that some guys use caffeine to avoid the resting stage of the adrenaline-rest cycle. They don't like how it feels to come down from a high, so they artificially stay up there as long as possible. It's fine to do that when you absolutely have to, but not as a regular coping strategy.

That Easter Sunday when Debbie and I pulled into the driveway of our home after all the services, I turned to her and remarked, "Do you realize that we had over 2,000 people at church this weekend?

Debbie looked at me and said without an ounce of excitement, "That's your dream. It's certainly not mine."

I may not be the smartest guy on the bus, but in that moment I realized, *Houston, we have a problem.* It slowly dawned on me that I'd been so focused on reaching the world for Christ that I'd neglected the most important people He put in my life. The church had become a rival girlfriend. Debbie didn't feel like she was a priority; she didn't feel cherished. I'd obviously had the problem for years, so proving my heart had changed took a long time. Trust is precious, and it can't be rebuilt easily or quickly. Debbie deserved much better than I'd given her. Thankfully, she was willing to work on this with me. I made some big improvements, and we're doing better than ever now.

It's almost trite to say that pastor's kids (PKs) get the worst of what happens in churches, and they often pay a high price for their parent's commitment to serve the church. I've certainly known kids whose father was a man of high character but got crosswise with the elders or deacons, and the turmoil flooded the whole family. But I've also seen children devastated by a parent's sins. The kids suffer ridicule, or at least guilt by association, and many of them are as deeply hurt as those their parents offended. I'd like to think that I'll never have to walk into a living room for a pastor to tell his wife and children about an affair, embezzling money, an addiction, or another disqualifying failure. . . . but I'm sure I haven't seen the last of those painful confessions.

I was on my way to the airport to fly to the nation's capital for a meeting when I got a call from a pastor who sounded desperate. He asked me to come so I could help him with a monumental problem—he'd been having an affair for almost a year, and he'd been outed by one of his elders. I changed my flight and flew to meet with him. Before I boarded the plane, I asked him to email me the church's constitution and bylaws so I'd know what I was walking into. He picked me up when I landed. We met with the elders, who had the authority and the will to fire him, effective immediately. I then went with him to tell his wife, and then his children, about his sin and the board's decision. His wife wept as hard as anyone I've ever heard. She *felt* betrayed because she *had been* betrayed. A whirlwind of questions—about the past, the present, and the future—flooded her mind, and there were few obvious answers. Two of the kids sat in stunned silence, but a daughter who was a junior in high school was perceptive enough to have guessed what had been happening. She had seen this day coming. She wasn't stunned and passive; she was furious. She hugged her mother and promised to be with her no matter what happened. Her gesture meant the world to her mom.

I met with the staff team. They were shocked by the news. I told them, "Things are changing here, and it's not happening tomorrow or next week. It's happening today." In the turmoil of the next few months, people in the church took sides, for the clear decision of the board to fire the pastor . . . or for letting the pastor apologize and stay in his role. Predictably, attendance and giving declined, so several staff members had to be let go. The pastor's failure had a dramatic, negative impact on his family, his team, the church, and the reputation of Christ in the community. For years, he had ignored the warning signs. Step by step, he got closer to the cliff, rationalizing every bad decision along the way.

In another situation, an executive pastor called to ask for my advice. He explained that his pastor, his best friend, had gone out with a woman while his wife was out of town. They met at a bar a long way from where the pastor lived, so he assumed he could keep it all quiet. That night, both of them got drunk, and when she invited him to her house, he accepted the invitation. They spent the night in sex and sleep. The next morning, he got up, got dressed, and went to the church office. He was sure no one would ever know. . . . but the woman had a pained conscience. She called the chairman of the elder board and asked him to meet with her. She told him the entire story. The board convened that day and removed the pastor from his position. His wife came home the next day and learned that her world had been turned upside down. The executive pastor asked, "Pastor Greg, what should I do?"

THE ENDURANCE FACTOR

I told him, "You're the ballast in the ship. Your job is to keep it steady in these stormy seas. Prepare your sermons for the next few weeks, and make them good ones. You'll be tempted to be preoccupied with all of the confusion, anger, and fear among the team and the people, but make sure you carve out time to think, pray, and prepare. They need you to be at your best."

Even if we've been leading effective church ministries for years, many of us aren't very good at telling ourselves the truth. Some of us beat ourselves bloody by focusing on every failure or slight from others, and even every *perceived* failure and slight— hello, paranoia. But others tell the story that "The rules don't apply to me," "I'm special. They need me," "I'm immune to temptation," "I don't really need boundaries or limitations," "I'd never do anything stupid," or "I'm indispensable. What would they do without me?" Excuses and rationalizations erode the early warning systems and set us up to make really bad decisions. We may not have an affair or embezzle money from the church, but we "die by a thousand cuts" as we drift toward self-condemnation and shame . . . or arrogance and an unquenchable thirst for power.

The hard but necessary truth is that we're deeply flawed and always vulnerable, but completely forgiven and totally adored by the Father. A Jewish rabbi commented, "A man should carry two stones in his pocket. On one should be inscribed, 'I am but dust and ashes.' On the other, 'For my sake was the world created.' And he should use each stone as he needs it."[11] Wise pastors carry the same two stones.

> **The hard but necessary truth is that we're deeply flawed and always vulnerable, but completely forgiven and totally adored by the Father.**

CHIP'S TAKE

It hurts when we see or hear about another pastor or leader taken out of the ministry by sin, behavior that misses the mark and falls short of what God expects. We're usually surprised and stunned. There's a collective sense that *we didn't see it coming* and *why weren't there warning signs*? Being a counselor is not just what I do. It's how I'm wired and it's hard to shut off. So when I'm around people, leaders or not, I'm watching and observing in different ways than most people are. It's not that I'm trying to catch people doing things wrong or psychoanalyze everyone. It's just that my radar is set to different settings and

---

11 Rabbi Bunam, quoted in Philip Yancey, *Reaching for the Invisible God* (Grand Rapids: Zondervan, 2000), p. 93.

sensitive to the personal and relational dynamics happening in the moment and what those dynamics tell us about the condition of the people involved.

When I attend a national pastor's conference, I do what counselors do: I observe people. I've met with enough pastors to know that many of them are totally dedicated to their calling for complicated reasons—they genuinely love and follow Jesus, but often, they're driven to prove themselves because their parents, primarily their fathers, didn't give them a firm foundation of love and affirmation. As I scan the room, I see a room full of orphans—men and women starved for affection and affirmation, and they look to people higher than themselves on the pecking order of success in their area of life and ministry to acknowledge that they belong in this room with these people. It can be as simple as eye contact and "Hello," or a two-minute conversation with someone who really seems interested in them. I watch them position themselves to be near leaders they respect, as if proximity validates their worth. Some positioning is for "business reasons," to get contacts or tap into resources, but most of it is "soul thirst." It's like they're walking around with an empty cup, hoping someone will pour a little water of attention into it, but the problem is everyone's trying to get their cup filled and few are operating from a full enough cup to focus on replenishing others.

In the green room, I see the same thirst from famous pastors, but most of them have become more sophisticated in hiding it. They get their significance from externals—performance, metrics, and notoriety—instead of the unquenchable love of God. They're acting like orphans, too, not beloved sons and daughters of the King. I want to tell the unknown people walking around the auditorium and the rockstars in the green room, "Hey, you have a Father who delights in you. He longs to fill not just your leaky cup, but your aching heart, to convince you that you can't earn security and significance. You already have it to the fullest! Know it, receive it, and delight in it." God, by His Word and His Spirit, says to us the things we desperately wished our own fathers said to us and about us: "You are My beloved son or daughter, and I'm so pleased with you. I love you more than you can ever know. You're a masterpiece to Me, My delight. And I want to shower My love on you all day every day . . . especially when you mess up. Don't think you can merit My love. It's a gift, pure and simple."

When I look at these leaders, I think of God speaking through Jeremiah when His people had gotten off track. He asked with obvious pain in His heart,

> Has any nation ever traded its gods for new ones, even though they are not gods at all? Yet my people have exchanged their glorious God for worthless idols! The heavens are shocked at such a thing and shrink back in horror and dismay," says the Lord. —Jeremiah 2:11-12, NLT

Then, with what I imagine is a blend of anger and deep sorrow, God gives His assessment of their problem: "For my people have done two evil things: They have abandoned me—the fountain of living water. And they have dug for themselves cracked cisterns that can hold no water at all!" (v. 13, NLT)

That's what I see in the lives of so many pastors: They've worked hard to dig cisterns, but they're cracked, so they leak. They keep trying to fill it with water so they can drink and be satisfied, but all their efforts leave them still thirsty. Oh, they try to convince themselves and others that all their frantic activity and posing gives them ultimate fulfillment, but somewhere deep in their souls, they know it's a lie. This passage in Jeremiah foreshadows when Jesus made a pronouncement in the Temple during a festival in John 7. During the days of the event, there were washings and sacrifices, feasts, and celebration. In a crescendo of intensity, everyone looked forward to the final day. At this dramatic moment, Jesus didn't just whisper to a few who were close to Him. He stood and shouted so everyone could hear!

> On the last day, the climax of the festival, Jesus stood and shouted to the crowds, "Anyone who is thirsty may come to me! Anyone who believes in me may come and drink! For the Scriptures declare, 'Rivers of living water will flow from his heart.'" (When he said "living water," he was speaking of the Spirit, who would be given to everyone believing in him.) —John 7:37-39, NLT

Isn't that what our hearts long for? Isn't He what really satisfies? It's not wrong to be thirsty. In fact, it's a necessary precondition to find the right drink. But stop drinking from broken cisterns, and in fact, stop digging them! Go to the source.

> **Our first calling is to Him and to the development of a rich, deep, ongoing, intimate relationship that touches us more deeply than any other relationship.**

It's so easy for our energy and attention to be drawn to and caught up in the endless pursuit of doing ministry well. We're rightfully committed to strategies, methods, and procedures that create opportunities for the lost to be found. But in all the hustle and bustle, have we, as leaders, forgotten that we teach what we know and reproduce what we are? If we've lost seeking God in our effort to serve Him, where does that leave those who follow us? Our first calling is to Him and to the development of a rich, deep, ongoing, intimate relationship that touches us more deeply than any other relationship.

The pastor of a large, blowing-and-going church brought me in to meet with him and his awesome team. We met a couple of times the first day I arrived. The next morning I was scheduled to speak to the entire staff. I had some cool notes and ideas I planned to share with them. As I was in my hotel room that night reaching to turn off the bedside light and go to sleep, I prayed, "Lord, forgive me. I didn't ask you if you have a word for this church and its leaders." Instantly, I sensed Him say, "They're so focused on the wineskins, they've neglected the wine." I knew exactly what He meant. The pastor and his team were devoted to fine-tuning the delivery system, the wineskins, but they didn't spend time delighting in the wine: God's grace, kindness, and love. Oh, they taught the doctrines and preached the message of grace, but their conversations with each other were far more—almost exclusively—about getting the delivery systems just right. Yes, it's important to make our events and services attractive and reach the community, but we have nothing to offer without the wine—a loving, passionate, engaging love affair with God. It's not just that particular pastor and that team. In many, many situations, church leaders invest their hearts and spend their energies on the wineskins. All you have to do is listen during a staff meeting. What's most important? What needs attention? What gets them excited? My friend Jeff Kapusta, a great pastor in Wilmington, North Carolina, said one time as we discussed this challenge, "We're so busy creating environments where others can experience God that we're not experiencing Him ourselves."

Are you DUI? Are you driving under the influence of our product, the true wine, or are we merely creating outstanding wineskins? If people follow you around for a week, would they see a passionate, tender heart for God and a genuine love for people, or would they see someone who is working really hard to create an environment where others can encounter God? If they asked you to describe the last genuine, heart-moving moment of connection with God, would you have to dredge up something that happened a year ago, or would it be yesterday? When was the last time you heard Him call you by name? When was the last time you laughed or cried in His presence?

Please don't get me wrong: I'm not advocating poorly planned or executed services and events. I've heard someone describe many church services today as "a Cold Play concert followed by a TED talk." Certainly, we want to do things with excellence, but the most attractive force in the universe is a life saturated in the grace God pours out on those who are hungry, lost, and hurting.

I learned from Bill Hull years ago from his book, *The Disciple-Making Pastor*,[12] that most pastors and church leaders are asking the wrong questions. We're overly focused on "how many?" and "how much?" The right question is: "what kind?" What kind of people is your ministry building and sending out into the world? During the last three years, we've had an opportunity to observe the fruit of our labors. Have we seen, and are we continuing to see, a culture infiltrated by followers of Jesus that carry His humble, loving grace and truth into a confused and hurting world? Or have we seen committed church-attending people who don't seem to realize you can be

12 Bill Hull, The Disciple-Making Pastor: Leading Others on the Journey of Faith (Grand Rapids, MI: Baker Books, 2007).

right and wrong at the same time? You can say the right thing in the wrong spirit, or the wrong thing in the right spirit. Neither of them will produce the desired result. Both of them will fail at representing Jesus to a blind and deceived people.

> The most attractive force in the universe is a life saturated in the grace God pours out on those who are hungry, lost, and hurting.

The church is a factory. We build a product that we send out into the world. What are we creating and sending? Remember—we teach what we know, but we reproduce what we are. If we want to reproduce disciples who have a vibrant, rich, overflowing relationship with God, it's pretty important that we have one ourselves.

Let me ask a few diagnostic questions:

- Does following you as a leader make me a better spouse, parent, and friend?
- Does following you make me more driven, or do you regularly point me to the wonder of God's love?
- Does following you make me feel better or worse about myself?

- In staff meetings, conferences, and church services, what do you celebrate? Is it "fast" and "big," or is it God's goodness and grace in using all kinds of people in very different ways?

All of us have blind spots, but we don't have to remain blind. When Martin Luther nailed the 95 theses to the church door at Wittenberg, the first one on the list read, "When our Lord and Master Jesus Christ said, 'Repent' (Matthew 4:17), he willed the entire life of believers to be one of repentance."[13] Repentance is the radical renewal and renovation of our thoughts, beliefs, and behaviors. It's God's work to incrementally conform us to the image of His Son from the inside out. When we begin to grasp the wonder of God's love, repentance is the way we reconnect with His kindness, forgiveness, and strength. Instead of running from repentance, we run toward it. Instead of waiting to repent when we've crashed, we can make a zillion mid-course corrections so we stay close to God's heart and His purposes.

Every decision costs us something. We choose this at the expense of pursuing that. When we choose hurry, big, wineskins, power, and success, we'll eventually pay a steep price. If we choose the love of the Father, we're deeply satisfied with Him, and to our surprise, He often gives us meaningful, effective ministries because people are drawn to the light and warmth coming from us. We use the wineskins to carry the wine to as many people as possible. The price we pay is that we're different, we measure ourselves by a different scoreboard.

13 "95 Theses," https://www.luther.de/en/95thesen.html

We define success and winning by a different standard. Some people didn't like Jesus because He rewrote the rules, and people around us may think we've quit the game we've all been playing. That's okay. We have.

When we begin to grasp the wonder of God's love, repentance is the way we reconnect with His kindness, forgiveness, and strength.

CHAPTER 4

THE LONG ROAD DOWN

GREG'S TAKE

In my career, I've met with many leaders who were at various stages of running out of gas. Some of them were still running fast, though their check-engine light was on; others were on fumes; and still others were facing physical, emotional, and relational collapse. It can happen to any of us. In an article in *Inc.*, the author distills research on burnout and lists twelve distinct and progressive stages:

1) The compulsion to prove yourself: Striving for excellence isn't the problem; it's the underlying motivation for our performance to convince others that we're valuable.

2) Working harder: But how much is enough?

3) Neglecting needs: Too busy to eat a healthy diet, too worried to sleep well, not enough energy for exercise.

4) Displacement of conflicts: Avoiding conflicts and difficult decisions.

5) Revision of values: Success becomes the ultimate aim—not honor, integrity, or compassion.

6) Denial of emerging problems: Instead of looking in the mirror to see the signs of increasing stress, we blame others and become cynical.

7) Withdrawal: Avoiding people because they may ask hard questions, looking for relief from an addictive behavior.

8) Odd behavioral changes: People notice the changes and are concerned.

9) Depersonalization: People are viewed as either tools or nuisances.

10) Inner emptiness: Lack of meaning and purpose, exaggerated emotions, and heightened desire to escape by using addictive substances or behaviors.

11) Depression: Feeling helpless, hopeless, and worthless.

12) Burnout syndrome: Physical, mental, emotional, and spiritual collapse.

The author concludes: "Symptoms of burnout range from mild but worrisome behaviors you probably encounter every day at work (perceiving colleagues as stupid, cynicism) to utter collapse. Obviously, you want to avoid the most severe ones, but the trick to doing that is to pay attention to more subtle signs rather than dismissing them as an unavoidable part of a hard-charging professional life."[14]

It's interesting that failure isn't necessarily a part of the slide toward burnout, but sometimes, amazing success is a part of it. Elijah's confrontation with the prophets of Baal on Mt. Carmel is one of the most dramatic scenes in the Scriptures. Imagine being in the grandstands to watch each side build a stone altar and ask for divine power to burn the sacrifice on it. The 450 prophets ". . . called on the name of Baal from morning until noon, saying, 'O Baal, answer us!' But there was no voice and no one answered." Elijah mocked them, asking if Baal might be in the bathroom, out of the office on a trip, or asleep. In response, the prophets tried even harder: "So they cried out with a loud voice, and cut themselves according to their custom with swords and lances until blood gushed out on them. When midday was past, they raved until the time of the offering of the *evening* sacrifice; but there was no voice, no one answered, and no one paid attention" (1 Kings 18:26, 28-29).

Elijah called the fans in the stands to come nearer. He rebuilt the altar (because the prophets' wild actions had knocked it down), dug a trench around it, put wood on the altar, and cut an ox in pieces on top of the wood. He instructed some who were nearby to pour a lot of water on the sacrifice and the wood and fill up the trench. Now he was ready. With the exhausted

---

14 Jessica Stillman, "The 12 Stages of Burnout, According to Psychologists," *Inc.*, August 2, 2017, https://www.inc.com/jessica-stillman/the-12-stages-of-burnout-according-to-psychologist.html.

and bleeding prophets and the mass of people looking on, Elijah prayed, "Answer me, LORD, answer me, so that this people may know that You, LORD, are God, and *that* You have turned their heart back" (v. 37). The historian takes us to the scene:

> Then the fire of the LORD fell and consumed the burnt offering and the wood, and the stones and the dust; and it licked up the water that was in the trench. When all the people saw this, they fell on their faces; and they said, "The LORD, He is God; the LORD, He is God!" Then Elijah said to them, "Seize the prophets of Baal; do not let one of them escape." So they seized them; and Elijah brought them down to the brook Kishon, and slaughtered them there. (vs. 38-40)

God had caused a drought in the land for three years, but at this moment, Elijah told the evil King Ahab to listen for the sound of a downpour. The king didn't believe him. Elijah went to the top of Mount Carmel, and looked out over the sea for a sign of a storm cloud, but there was nothing. He sent his servant back seven times, and after the seventh, the servant reported, ". . . Behold, a cloud as small as a man's hand is coming up from the sea" (v. 44). Elijah sent word to Ahab to get ready to be drenched, and sure enough, the heavens opened in a torrent.

If there's ever been a dramatically successful day of ministry, this was it!

Ahab told Queen Jezebel all that happened that day, but she wasn't threatened in the least. She sent word to the prophet,

"So may the gods do to me and more so, if *by* about this time tomorrow I do not make your life like the life of one of them" (1 Kings 19:2). Elijah had stood tall against 450 men who challenged him and his God, but one woman terrified him! He ran all the way to Beersheba in Judah—well over one hundred miles. He left his servant there, and he walked another day into the wilderness, a place he hoped no one could find him. There, his discouragement overwhelmed him (he obviously didn't understand the adrenaline cycle!), and he begged God to kill him: "Enough! Now, LORD, take my life, for I am no better than my fathers" (v. 4).

God didn't answer Elijah's prayer, at least, not in the way he expected. Elijah needed some sleep, and he only woke up when an angel touched him and gave him something to eat. He was still exhausted, so he went to sleep again. The angel woke him a second time to give him another meal, and then Elijah walked to Horeb, which is in today's Saudi Arabia. The Lord showed up and asked,

> What are you doing here, Elijah? And the prophet poured out his self-pity: "I have been very zealous for the LORD, the God of armies; for the sons of Israel have abandoned Your covenant, torn down Your altars, and killed Your prophets with the sword. And I alone am left; and they have sought to take my life." (vs. 9-10)

THE ENDURANCE FACTOR

"I'm all alone . . . and everyone is against me!" That's a sentiment echoed by many stressed pastors who are sliding through the stages of burnout.

God told Elijah to stand on the mountain, "And behold, the Lord was passing by!" (v. 11) First, a powerful wind tore the mountains and broke rocks into pieces. An earthquake shook the earth, and then a fire ravaged what was left, but the Lord wasn't in any of these dramatic signs. Finally, a gentle wind blew, and God asked again, "What are you doing here, Elijah?" (v. 13) It seems the prophet was still filled with resentment and self-pity because he answered the same way as before: "I'm all alone, and everyone is against me!"

God didn't try to correct him. He just gave him his next assignment: go to Damascus, anoint a new king over Aram, a new king over Israel, and Elisha as his replacement. But God assured him that, in fact, he wasn't alone: "Yet I will leave seven thousand in Israel, all the knees that have not bowed to Baal and every mouth that has not kissed him" (v. 18).

As we saw in an earlier chapter, every event—positive and negative—adds a measure of stress to our lives. If we don't limit the accumulation, and if we fail to resolve the buildup, we can crater. Elijah's stunning mountaintop successes, all in one day, made him vulnerable to a colossal valley of physical, emotional, and spiritual depletion. In that condition, God carefully orchestrated exactly what he needed: rest, food, and a fresh sense of His presence and power.

I've seen countless church leaders like Elijah. No, they haven't called down fire from heaven, slain 450 enemies of God, and shattered a seven-year drought, but even though God is doing wonderful things in their churches, these leaders have become depressed, cynical, grumpy, detached, and lonely. They have only one lens to look through, the one that makes everything look like a threat or a disaster. They have only one way to relate to people, as those who have let them down. One pastor lamented, "I thought our church would be further along at this point. I don't know what's wrong. Maybe it's me."

Another one complained, "My staff team is driving me crazy. Were they incompetent already, or did I make them incompetent?"

A pastor commented, "I'm exhausted. When I see people on my team laughing, I resent them."

Another confided, "I'm not sure I can go on. I've given it everything I've got, and it's just not enough."

You'd think their churches were completely barren of any spiritual movement, but that's not the case. In almost every situation, people are coming to Christ and God is working to shape them into His image, but these leaders can't see it. They may not have run to Beersheba, but they've run from the reality that God is still at work in and through them.

Loneliness is a huge problem for pastors, and the pattern is predictable: when we're cynical, we withdraw, and when we're irritable, the people around us withdraw. It's a package deal. In both ways, loneliness persists and becomes more acute.

THE ENDURANCE FACTOR

A range of childhood traumas—from relatively mild to extreme—is a contributing factor in the lives of many church leaders. For me, the imprinting of my parents was very positive, but some painful church experiences are also stored in my memory banks. In the churches where my father and grandfather pastored, the deacons often were the power center. They sometimes believed, "We were here before you came, and we'll be here after you've gone. This is our church, not yours." I overheard enough conversations around our dinner table about the demands of those in power that I was afraid to navigate those waters. As Seacoast grew, we realized we needed more structure, but I didn't want any written document that might give too much power to other people. . . . so I resisted writing and implementing them for thirteen years. I couldn't articulate my anxiety during those years, but later, as I reflected on it, I saw that I was afraid that if bylaws were written and a structure put in place, someone would find a way to arbitrarily remove me from the church I loved—the way the deacons had treated my father and my grandfather.

Finally, I was able (barely) to overcome my emotional hurdles, and we implemented bylaws for the church. We wrote them in a way that helps pastors lead and enables elders to play a supportive, protective role. Our structure gives clear authority, responsibility, and accountability for every role, and it leans toward staff leadership. It provides guidelines for instances when a pastor goes off the rails for one reason or another. I've found that when these things are clearly written, everyone involved knows their lane and can stay in it more easily. Yes, I know different denominations and affiliated churches have varied methods of polity, but this one works for us. By the way, whenever I hear someone claim, "Well, *our* church government is *the* biblical one," I'm somewhat skeptical. There are certainly biblical principles, but they can be applied in several different, workable structures.

Far too often, bylaws are written only after a pastoral disaster, so the next leader comes in under the structure that's a reaction to the last pastor. It's like someone who gets a divorce and holds his next spouse accountable for the mistakes of the previous one. It's not fair and it doesn't work.

What does church polity have to do with unmitigated stress? Sometimes nothing, often a lot. The way our systems are set up can bring us into regular contact with people who care about us, not just about our metrics. Isolation is one of the chief accelerators of burnout. A workable polity should establish strong relationships—not just for accountability when someone has gone off a cliff, but to keep people running well on the right road. (On a sidenote, I think congregations would do well to include soul care for pastors in the budget, in the same way we budget for missions, buildings, and other necessary ministry things.)

Isolation is one of the chief accelerators of burnout.

THE ENDURANCE FACTOR

The final stage of burnout is unmistakable—it's hard to deny it when you're so far gone that you can't function. The goal of this chapter is to help people see the warning signs so they can stop the downward drift . . . before it's too late. These signs include physical issues such as insomnia, exhaustion, eating too much or too little, frequent headaches, and digestive problems. Quite often increasing levels of stress are the product of compounded problems, including work stress, financial problems, relational disruptions, caring for aging parents, recent relocations, and changes in friendships. Soon, the powerful combination of factors makes us feel like life is out of control, nobody understands, and worse, nobody cares. That's what Elijah concluded . . . even after one of the most gloriously successful days in history!

CHIP'S TAKE

There is a certain exercise I do almost every time I go to a church to work with the staff for the first time. It's kind of fun and it seems to get the point across and get the conversation going in the right direction. I tell them I want to talk to them about a parable, not found in Scripture, that carries a great deal of wisdom and insight about how to LIVE WELL and FINISH STRONG in every area of life. I explain to them that I'm going to need their help and their participation. I ask them to be thinking as we're going through the parable about life principles and insights they could draw from it. I typically get a surprised response when I pull out an old, familiar children's book, *The Three Little Pigs*.[15] As we begin, I explain the parts they will play. I ask the men to be the pigs and the women to be the wolves. I explain that I need them to ham it up when we get to their parts in the story. It's usually quite animated as they follow along and compete in being the most animated and energetic in saying their lines.

The story is about three little pigs that are different in the way that they approach launching their lives into this big world. There's a lazy pig, a playful pig, and a smart pig. Each of them builds a house based on their unique wiring and makeup. Here's how the story describes what they build.

> *The first little pig was a lazy little pig. He built the simplest kind of house so he could have time to rest. His house was made of straw. It was not very strong. The second little pig was a playful little pig. He built his house quickly so he could go out and play. His house was made of sticks. It was not very strong. The third little pig was the smartest pig of all. He listened carefully to his mother's advice and built a strong house of bricks."*

We all know what happened next. The big, bad wolf came and knocked on each pig's door. It's fun to hear the staff play their part in reenacting what the wolf and the pig say. To each of the little pigs, the wolf says, "Little pig, little pig, let me come in." All of the pigs replied, "Not by the hair of my chinny-chin-chin." The wolf's response is, "Then I'll huff and

---

15 Harold M. Goralnick, *The Three Little Pigs* (Totowa, NJ: Grandreams USA, 1999).

THE ENDURANCE FACTOR

I'll puff and I'll blow your house in." At the first two houses, the lazy pig's and the playful pig's, the wolf huffs and puffs, and blows their houses down. But when he gets to the third little pig's house the same things are said, but when he huffs and puffs and he puffs and huffs, he can't blow the brick house down. The wolf gets angry, climbs on the roof, slides down the chimney, and ends up being part of their soup for lunch. It's typically a lot of fun watching the men and women imitate children's' versions of a pig's voice and a wolf's voice.

The really cool part is when the people on the team begin to share the life principles they saw in the story, quite often they have brilliant observations. What observations would you make? The observations in the room range from the very spiritual and obvious: the wolf is the devil, listen to your parents, build a strong foundation, to the not so obvious, such as the brother who built well is where others run when they encounter trouble. I'm always impressed with the variety and creativity of the thinking that drives their responses.

When they've finished, I share some of my thoughts on this parable:

> *What you build will be tested and you don't know the quality of what you've built until it is tested. What if the wolf is time? Time will reveal if what you've built in the short run is still standing in the long run. Your inner reality creates, shapes, and defines your outer reality. Who you are on the inside determines what you build on the outside. You can't*

consistently live in a way that is inconsistent with the way you see yourself. Whoever's words define you is your god.

Your inner reality shapes your outer reality. The inner reality of the first two pigs made them vulnerable to the threat of the wolf. In other words, their inner wiring dictated the kind of house they built. Our behavior is always a function of what we think about ourselves. If someone doesn't believe he's valuable and loved, he'll either act in ways that seek attention or withdraw into hiding. I have observed that people would rather be right than happy. In other words, living in a way that's consistent with the internal narrative, even if it's cruel and demeaning, is easier than changing that narrative. The story of the three little pigs highlights the point that a great start is admirable; a great finish is epic.

I always think about the parable of the sower whenever I read or discuss *The Three Little Pigs*.[16] Here it is from the Gospel of Mark:

> Listen to this! Behold, the sower went out to sow; as he was sowing, some seed fell beside the road, and the birds came and ate it up. Other seed fell on the rocky ground where it did not have much soil; and immediately it sprang up because it had no depth of soil. And after the sun had risen, it was scorched; and because it had no root, it withered away. Other seed fell among the thorns, and the thorns came up and choked it, and

16 Goralnick, The Three Little Pigs.

THE ENDURANCE FACTOR

> it yielded no crop. Other seeds fell into the good soil, and as
> they grew up and increased, they yielded a crop and produced
> thirty, sixty, and a hundredfold. —Mark 4:3-8

In this parable, there are four soils that each have a different ending. They all heard the word, but only one of the four permanently profited from what they heard. The others began the journey but did not finish well. Let me give you some sanctified psychology on how I use this parable to understand and work with myself and others. I hope this will help you in areas where you struggle. It will also help you understand why others have their story interrupted and don't finish well.

The first soil, by the roadside, is someone who's half in and half out. They're beginning the journey but haven't fully committed to it. The second soil is where the seed was sown on rocky ground. Which was there first, the seed or the rocks? The third soil is where the seed was sown among the thorns. Which was there first, the seed or the thorns? In both of these cases the seed was sown on the ground with what I would call "pre-existing conditions." In other words, the condition of the ground determined the penetration and progress of the seed that was sown into it. Jesus explains in Matthew 13 that the soil is the heart of the person. Hidden in this parable is the awesome insight that the condition of a person's heart when they are in the presence of God, listening to his word, determines the degree to which they are able to receive, apply, and benefit from that word. When we've experienced hurt and trauma (who hasn't?), and our heart is wounded and untrusting, it affects the way we see and hear what God is trying to say to us. When our lives are filled with the pursuit of things, even good things, it can choke out our passion and pursuit of God and His best for us.

In the progression of the parable, I believe the rocky soil represents hearts that have been wounded, and the thorns represent desires and ambitions. The thorns are misguided passions, a self-absorbed agenda, what we might call "idols" of power, pleasure, and popularity—pursuits that can seem more attractive than the love and blessings of God because everywhere we look, those things are promoted and celebrated as the highest, most desirable and fulfilling things on earth! But make no mistake: success can be just as mesmerizing as lust. The blessing of God is wonderful, but success can become the biggest weed in our garden.

> When our lives are filled with the pursuit of things, even good things, it can choke out our passion and pursuit of God and His best for us.

THE ENDURANCE FACTOR

What's one area of your life that you know God wants to work on? It's a simple question that most people can answer immediately. It might be their weight, anger, anxiety, fear, depression, exaggerating the truth, self-pity, resentment, the refusal to forgive, refusing to ever admit they're wrong, or a bad habit that has plagued them for a long time. Why do you struggle with that aspect of your life when your friends struggle with something completely different? Why are some things easy for others and hard for us? How did each of us become the people we are today? How did each of us develop into a person who has our unique strengths and weaknesses, personality type, work ethic, social skills, emotional challenges, and other things that make us who we are and determine what comes easily and what is difficult for us? Do you agree that we are all very different and that we struggle with different things? Let's talk about why.

Are all people created equal? That's a tricky question. Let me alter it to make it easier to answer. Are all people created *equal in value?* I'm pretty sure most of us would whole-heartedly agree that we are. Are all people created *equal in preparation and placement for success in life?* I hope you would agree that the answer to that question is "no."

Did you pick your parents? Did you pick the family you were born into? Do you remember a time when God came to you when you were a disembodied spirit and asked you if you would be the son or daughter of your particular parents? Did you fill out a preference sheet?

Did your placement in a particular family with all the other things that went with it have any effect on the person that you are, the opportunities you enjoyed, and the unique challenges that you faced?

I have come to believe that about two-thirds of what makes each of us the person we are is decided by factors over which we had no choice or capacity to challenge. I believe there are three things that have the greatest influence and impact on shaping who we have become. Those three things are:

- Genetic, multi-generational predisposition
- Early life imprints
- Our life choices

Does that mean we aren't responsible for the current state of our lives? My answer is "yes" and "no." You may not be responsible for the way that you are, but . . . you are responsible for changing the way you are. I want you to imagine two households on the same street. In one there's a baby about three months old sleeping in a crib right next to the parents' bed. When that baby wakes up in the middle of the night, both parents wake up and fight over who has the privilege of tending to their beloved daughter's needs. Right down the street there's a baby in its crib, crying in absolute terror. The baby has not had its diaper changed in two days. The mother is passed out on the couch in the living room from drinking and drugs. The father is nowhere to be found. Are those babies being equally valued and prepared for a great life? What are they "learning" about the world into which they've been born? One is learning,

"This is a friendly, caring place, and there are two big creatures that respond to me when I need it." The other baby is learning, "The world is a scary place, and there's no one I can trust." Is that going to affect these children as they become adults?

> **The greatest obstacles between you and the future you want are inside of you, not outside.**

These two scenarios may seem extreme, but both happen. It really happened in the neighborhood where I grew up. The point is that various factors, forces, and experiences—both good and bad—have shaped the person you are today. As we describe these factors and their impacts, ask God to give you insight into how your early life and treatment you received by the most important people in the world to you affected your development. The greatest obstacles between you and the future you want are inside of you, not outside. Your thoughts, beliefs, and behaviors determine the outcomes of your life. By far, most of the thoughts and beliefs that determine our behavior were learned and stored in our subconscious before we were able to choose them or challenge them. I want to give you a fairly simple way to look at and think about how you developed into the person that you are.

As I pursued my master's degree in counseling, I was exposed to different counseling models and theories that addressed four important questions. Your answers to these questions make up your "Theory of Human Development," which should feed into your "model of ministry," so your philosophy and strategy for helping people grow into the full potential that God has for them. The four questions are:

1) How do we develop as individuals?

2) How did God design us to work?

3) What can go wrong in our development?

4) How do we repair the damage?

I am committed to trying to make concepts as simple as possible. Here's my shot at explaining how you and I become the people that we are. Different authors may identify a hundred factors that shape who we are and how we respond to people and situations, but I have whittled them down to three that play major roles in our becoming the unique individuals that we are. Here we go.

The first factor is *Genetic, Multi-Generational Predisposition*. Did you get to pick your family? Do you remember being a disembodied spirit who had the opportunity to look at all the families in the world and say, "I pick them"? Did God come to you and say, "Chipper, how would you like to be the sixth of seven children of Leroy and Emily Judd, who live on 70 South Nicolas Drive in Tonawanda, New York?" Did you fill out a preference sheet: "I want a dad who is warm and strong, handsome, has a lot of money, and a mother who is gentle, smart, and funny"? The answer is obvious, but it's a setup for an important point: If you didn't get to pick your family, then the vast majority of who you are—genetics and environment/nature and nurture—were outside of your ability to choose. This means you can't take credit for the good traits that were passed down to you, and it's not automatically your fault that you struggle with certain issues. God warned Moses, "For I, the LORD your God, am a jealous God, inflicting the punishment of the fathers on the children, even on the third and the fourth *generations* of those who hate Me, but showing favor to thousands, to those who love Me and keep My commandments" (Deuteronomy 5:9).

It's very important to recognize that God doesn't visit *the sins* of the fathers onto the children. It's *the iniquity* that is transmitted from one generation to the next. We aren't responsible for the sins of our parents, but we are affected by their iniquities. The word *iniquity* means to be bent or crooked. In other words, we inherit the tendency toward certain behavior. Think about things you've seen repeated in the generations of families you know, things like addiction, anger, depression, and abuse, as well as healthy, productive attributes. The presence of unhealthy patterns in our ancestors doesn't mean we will automatically have the same issue, but we will be affected by their issues. When you look back only a couple of generations, it's often easy to see recurring patterns of anxiety, depression, divorce, abuse, addiction, and abandonment, as well as health problems like weight, diabetes, heart disease, some cancers, and a range of other genetically passed concerns. Some mental health problems, such as bipolar disorder and depression, are known to have strong genetic links.

The second factor shaping who we have become is *Early-Life Imprints*. Picture a young boy standing in front of a stove with a red hot burner. His mother says, "Johnny, don't touch that stove." When does that piece of advice from Mom become real to Johnny? When he puts his hand on the stove and gets burned, right? That's an imprint. An imprint is an experience combined with an emotion that leaves a lasting mark on a person's understanding of how life works.

$$Experience + Emotion = Imprint$$

Imprints are the subconscious meaning we attach to everything, and they affect our emotions and responses to life. In childhood we form imprints for everything. We have imprints for every aspect of life: intimacy, risk, handling fear, relating to friends, confidence, and on and on. Much of who we are and how we respond is the result of the experiences and emotions we had when we were young. Imprints operate from outside of our conscious awareness and they're really fast. We don't have to consciously tap into them; they're riveted to our souls and form our deepest, subconscious conceptions of the world. Those of us who grew up with "good enough parents" have positive imprints that help us embrace God's love and enable good traits like our diligence to work hard, tell the truth, and care for others, but I've talked to plenty of men and women whose negative imprints consume them.

Negative imprints often hide behind a network of coping strategies. We do anything and everything to keep from feeling the pain again. We may work exceptionally hard to prove ourselves to others, never admitting failure or defeat, and fiercely resisting any criticism. Or we may strive to please people. We become chameleons, changing our words and behavior to impress the person standing in front of us at the moment. Or we may become adept at "hiding in plain sight," withdrawing emotionally or physically to avoid any chance of feeling threatened in any way.

It's important to realize that most of our imprints occurred within the first three years of life, and certainly by the time we were seven. They remain in place until they are challenged and changed. We didn't get to pick our genetic predispositions, and we didn't have a menu of early imprints we could choose from. We were stamped with them without our ability to accept or reject them.

The third factor shaping who we've become is *Our Life Choices*. We had no options for the first two—genetic predisposition and early-life imprints—but we have great responsibility over this last one. In Paul's letter to the Romans, he explains that our choices define our loyalties: "Do you not know that *the one* to whom you present yourselves *as* slaves for obedience, you are slaves of *that same one* whom you obey, either of sin resulting in death, or of obedience resulting in righteousness?" (Romans 6:16)

Anything we say "yes" to, especially repeated over time, grows in power, and the things we say "no" to weaken and have less impact. The principle is true for alcohol, anger, laziness, overeating, or any other debilitating, destructive habits, and it's also valid in developing skills such as telling the truth, discipline, compassion, and the rest of the Christian virtues.

Even if the imprinting from childhood has been painful and destructive, we're not helpless and hopeless. God has given us the choice to enter into a process to change our thoughts, attitudes, and behavior . . . and even our brains. In an amazing gift of God, our brains have the capacity for *neuroplasticity*, the ability to change structure and function. As we bring our anguish to God, in the context of at least one wise and supportive person, we gradually grieve the losses we suffered, forgive the ones who hurt us, and heal in the deepest recesses of our hearts.

A pastor asked me to help him with a deep-seated, recurring problem: his volcanic anger. He told me, "I don't know what comes over me. I seem to be doing fine in addressing a problem, but then the lid blows off. I yell at the person in front of me. I know I hurt them terribly, and I feel horrible about it. I apologize, but I know better than to promise that it won't happen again." As we talked, I asked about his childhood. He told me about his father's rages. He explained that his dad blew up over seemingly insignificant things, but he ignored genuinely threatening situations. "It was totally irrational," the pastor said as he shook his head in disbelief. He soon understood that his outbursts were the product of genetic predispositions, powerful imprints from his childhood, and his own poor choices in failing to address his anger in appropriate ways. For him and many others, the solution isn't as simple as "Just stop it," or "Just pray about it." He had tried for years to curb his explosive anger, and he had asked God again and again to take it away. Nothing changed, but now he had a new choice to enter into the long and effective process of emotional, psychological, relational, and spiritual healing.

I met with an attractive woman who genuinely believed she was ugly. Throughout her childhood, her mother was never satisfied with her appearance: her clothes, her hair, her weight, her complexion . . . everything was up for critique every day. Before long, she lost confidence in herself, and she believed she couldn't make any choice that was good enough. It was no longer just about her appearance—she felt defective in every aspect of her life. She tried exceptionally hard to prove herself by her sharp clothes, her perfect hair, her workouts to keep her figure, and her diligence at work. She wanted to be sure there was no way anyone could ever say another critical word to her, but of course, she lived in secret fear all day every day that her striving wasn't enough. As we talked, she admitted that her mother's constant, critical observations, coupled with her father's emotional detachment, had been painful, but until that day, she hadn't realized how pervasive and destructive their impact had been. She wept in pain and righteous anger. She was ready for the process of healing.

The vast majority of leaders don't realize the power they have over the people on their teams. I talk to pastors who tell me, "I listen to their ideas. I see myself as just one of the people on the team as we talk about new projects or challenges."

"But you're not 'just one of the people on the team,'" I explain. "When you give your opinion or suggestion, whether it's at the beginning or the end, the discussion is over." Quite often, pastors look puzzled at this point, so I continue. "They want one thing from you more than any other: validation. How do they get it? By pleasing you. When you say you like something or are for this program, the interaction is over. They conclude that the best way to get the validation they crave is to agree with you. Their goal then is to get you what you want. That's what they're paid to do, and that's their best shot at getting your approval."

My father only told me twice that he loved me by the time I was seventeen. He wasn't good at expressing emotions, and he liked my brother more than me. He didn't love him more, but he had more in common and enjoyed their relationship more. When he was frustrated with me, which was pretty often, he told me, "You're lazy, and you'll never amount to anything." That message, and the facial expression that accompanied it, were deeply imprinted on my soul. As a young adult, when I was presented with opportunities, I daydreamed and planned to take advantage of them, but sooner or later, a voice inside my head would say, "*Yeah, but you'd better not even try. You're too lazy, so you won't stick with it.*" It was like a switch was flipped—I changed from eager optimism to hopeless discouragement. In the face of golden opportunities, I self-sabotaged many of them.

> **When our hunger for intimacy, affirmation, and meaning isn't met, it's like going to the grocery store when we're hungry—we buy a lot of stuff that we don't need and isn't good for us.**

As I grew up, I was desperate to please my father to win his affirmation, and I was terrified that I'd hear those condemning words again. Naturally, this affected my view of all authority figures, not just my dad. I felt insecure and inferior, so I over-compensated. I didn't just join in as people told stories; my story had to be better than yours. I tried everything to stand out and be noticed, but I felt like a fraud.

When our hunger for intimacy, affirmation, and meaning isn't met, it's like going to the grocery store when we're hungry—we buy a lot of stuff that we don't need and isn't good for us. That's what I see in the lives of many people who come to me for help: they're trying to satisfy legitimate hunger with junk food.

The long road down happens when we, like the first two little pigs, aren't alert to the dangers around us. We can all slide down that road. None of us is immune to the wolf's schemes. If we understand the internal dynamics put into motion when we were children, we'll have more insight about why we think and act the way we do, and we'll have clearer choices about our futures. Security and significance may have been elusive in the past, but the Father is waiting for us with open arms.

CHAPTER 5
LOOKIN' FOR LOVE

GREG'S TAKE

Each Sunday when we stand up and share God's Word, we're completely exposed, vulnerable, and for many of us, fragile. It feels so good when someone comes up to us later and says, "Pastor, what you said today went right to my heart. I really needed it. Thank you so much." Sometimes people have said that to me, and then they went on to explain how the Holy Spirit had specifically applied it to an issue they're facing. . . . and on more than one occasion, the application had nothing to do with what I'd said in the sermon. The Spirit was willing to use my words in a way I wasn't expecting in the least.

THE ENDURANCE FACTOR

But it's not always like that. One Sunday when I preached at the church I pastored in a little farming community in Illinois, my words produced a very different reaction. In my preparation and study, it all made perfect sense, but in the middle of my message, I suddenly had no idea where I was going with it. Conflicting concepts were swirling in my mind. I needed to grab one and go with it, but which one? I muddled through. I hoped it was better than I thought it was. Maybe God used it somehow. After the service, I stood in the lobby shaking hands when an old farmer came up to me and said, "Pastor, I really like you, but for the life of me, I didn't know what in the hell you were talking about today." I completely understood. I felt exactly the same way.

I know from experience that it's easy to become addicted to the applause of the crowd. It's perfectly fine for people to appreciate us and our messages, but we cross a line when we have to have it to feel okay about ourselves. When we crave it, it moves Jesus off the throne of our hearts.

My parents were wonderful people, but they were far from perfect. Like everyone else, I grew up with some childhood hurts. One of the recurring wounds, like ripping a bandage off a wound time after time, was the teaching (or at least the strong impression) that God is perpetually angry with me. I was sure that every time God looked at me, He had a frown on His face. We were taught that we could lose our salvation, but how big a sin did it take? Was this one over the line? How about that one? This belief caused me to suffer from "Rapture fear." I was terrified that when Jesus came back, I'd be left behind . . . which was the title of a set of books and a movie series that only reinforced my fears. As a boy, when it got really quiet in our house, I was afraid the Rapture had happened, and I was alone in the house. Sometimes at night, when it was especially quiet, I would sneak into my parents' bedroom to see if they were still there. I always went to my mom's side of the bed because I was sure she was going. . . . I wasn't quite as sure about my dad.

> **It's perfectly fine for people to appreciate us and our messages, but we cross a line when we have to have it to feel okay about ourselves. When we crave it, it moves Jesus off the throne of our hearts.**

As a pastor, my theology has deepened and broadened, so my childhood fears of being left behind at the Rapture were gradually put to rest, but I still had the nagging suspicion that God tolerated me at best and was continuously upset with me at worst. From the pulpit, I taught the unmerited and unlimited grace of God with all my might, but I must have thought God dearly loved other people, not me.

Soon after I met Chip, he shared his focus on recognizing, receiving, and resting in the Father's love. I knew all the verses about His love, but for some reason, Chip's grasp made more of an impact on me than anything I'd ever heard. I thought back to the many times I felt like God was angry with me because I'd missed a devotional time or failed in some other way to follow the prescription of being a "good Christian," and it hit me: I was making a much bigger deal of it than God was! His love wasn't (and isn't) contingent on me jumping through all the hoops. He just loves me. Yes, He wants to spend time with me, but to show me His love, not to blast me for not opening my Bible the day before. (It may seem odd to some people that a pastor would think this way, but at least a few of you know exactly what I'm talking about.) I have begun a daily practice to refocus my mind and heart as soon as I wake up. I say out loud: "This is going to be a great day because I have a Father who's crazy about me and has a wonderful plan for my life!"

Some people naturally wake up full of joy and optimism every day. I don't understand them at all. I often wake up grumpy, so I have to fight for my joy every day. When I operate from a secure place in the Father's love, I can receive the praise of people without it meaning too much, and I can receive criticism without being crushed. The thirst for approval isn't negotiable—it's standard equipment for every human being—but we can function *from* approval or *for* approval. The prepositions make a world of difference. If we live for the approval of others, we pose to impress them, we shade the truth to avoid being found deficient, and we demand that they appreciate us, or else. That's not loving them the way Jesus loves us!

God's love fills the gaping hole in our souls. Everything else is a counterfeit, a substitute that promises to fill us but can't deliver. Many people recoil at the term "idolatry," but it doesn't mean bowing in front of little stone statues in New Guinea. In his book, *Counterfeit Gods*, pastor and author Tim Keller explains, "An idol is anything more important to you than God. Anything that absorbs your heart and imagination more than God. Anything you seek to give you what only God can give. Anything that is so central and essential to your life, that should you lose it, your life would feel hardly worth living." Almost anything or anyone can take God's rightful place in our hearts: success, pleasure, approval, power, control, wealth, acclaim . . . the list is endless. It's what occupies our daydreams when we have nothing else to think about, and it's what inflames fear and anger when anyone gets in the way of acquiring it. When our idol is fulfilled, we feel superior to others; when it isn't, we feel ashamed, less than, and worthless. . . . and we resent those who get in our way. For instance, if the approval of people means too much to us, we'll think about it day and night, reliving compliments and dreading even a frown from someone whose smile we depend on. Keller explains how we respond when we don't get what we desperately want:

THE ENDURANCE FACTOR

*No person, not even the best one can give your soul
all it needs. . . . this cosmic disappointment and disillusionment is there in all of life, but we especially feel
it in the things in which we set our hopes. When you
finally realize this, there are four things you can do:
You can blame the things that are disappointing you
and try to move on to better ones (that's the way of
continued idolatry and spiritual addiction), you can
blame yourself and beat yourself (that's the way of
self-loathing and shame), you can blame the world
(that's how you get hard, cynical, and empty), or you
can reorient the entire focus of your life on God.[17]*

God has made us so that only He can fill the hole in our
hearts. When we pursue other things that promise to fit, they're
like BBs rolling around in a boxcar. . . . they leave us empty,
confused, and longing for more. It's not too much to say that
whatever we value supremely becomes nothing less than the
object of our worship. Novelist David Foster Wallace wasn't a
believer, but he put his finger on this point in his commencement
address at Kenyon College:

*If you worship money and things—if they are
where you tap real meaning in life—then you will
never have enough. Never feel you have enough.
It's the truth. Worship your own body and beauty
and sexual allure and you will always feel ugly, and
when time and age start showing, you will die a*

17 Tim Keller, *Counterfeit Gods* (New York: Hodder & Stoughton, 2010), p. xvii.

million deaths before they finally plant you. On one
level, we all know this stuff already—it's been codi-
fied as myths, proverbs, clichés, bromides, epigrams,
parables: the skeleton of every great story. The trick
is keeping the truth up front in daily consciousness.
Worship power—you will feel weak and afraid, and
you will need ever more power over others to keep
the fear at bay. Worship your intellect, being seen
as smart—you will end up feeling stupid, a fraud,
always on the verge of being found out.[18]

Do you think the idea of "worshipping" those things is exag-
geration? It's not. We worship what's most important to us—we
think about it, we plan for it, we fear losing it, and we long for
it above other things. . . . that's worship! When we realize our
hearts are too wrapped up in anything that's not the Father's
love (and at least from time to time, we will), what can we do?
Some of us believe we need to blast ourselves for being such
awful Christians, and others tell ourselves, "Just stop it!" Neither of these produces anything but guilt and shame. There's
another way . . . a much better way. Many years ago, the Scot-
tish minister Thomas Chalmers wrote an article (probably a
transcript of one of his sermons) to explain that it doesn't help
to call our present affections—bigness and quickness, but also
wealth, fame, power, and intelligence—worthless. "The only
way to dispossess [the human heart] of an old affection is by the

---

18 David Foster Wallace, "This Is Water," Kenyon College Commencement, quoted in
www.theguardian.com/books/2008/sep/20/fiction

expulsive power of a new one." We don't change, he explained, by trying to clamp down on our misplaced passions; but we change with supernatural power when we rivet our attention on God's amazing grace, so that it becomes "the expulsive power of a new affection."[19]

The statement I say each morning reminds me of the powerful new affection that crowds out lesser ones—and God knows, I need to be reminded every day! The change is remarkable. Even as someone who taught God's love and the grace poured out in Jesus, it was too easy to teach it but not experience it, at least not deeply enough. In this book, *Return of the Prodigal Son*, Henri Nouwen describes the sweeping change that happens in us when God's love is all we want and when we discover it's all we need:

> *Your true identity is as a child of God. This is the identity you have to accept. Once you have claimed it and settled in it, you can live in a world that gives you much joy as well as pain. You can receive the praise as well as the blame that comes to you as an opportunity for strengthening your basic identity, because the identity that makes you free is anchored beyond all human praise and blame. You belong to God, and it is as a child of God that you are sent into the world.*[20]

---

19 Thomas Chalmers, "The Expulsive Power of a New Affection," https://www. christianity.com/wiki/history/the-expulsive-power-of-a-new-affection-11627257.html.

20 Henri Nouwen, *Return of the Prodigal Son* (New York: Doubleday, 1992), p. 9.

A security "beyond all human praise or blame"? A life that isn't shattered by criticism and isn't always desperately thirsty for validation? Is that even possible? Yes, it certainly is, but we have to do the hard work of going deeper, ever deeper, into the love of the Father. Jesus paid a brutal price to bring us back to God, but He paid it gladly, willingly, lovingly. And the Father was delighted at the prospect of calling us His own. Our response of faith would be impossible without the tender calling of the Holy Spirit, awakening our longing to be known and loved by the ultimate authority, the Good Shepherd, and the Father of lights.

> **We need to resign from the position of general manager of the universe and let God do what only He can do.**

One of the complicating factors for pastors is the inability to delineate responsibilities—not between the pastor and staff members, but between the pastor and God. We want our churches to grow, and we obsess over the size of every service, heaping praise or blame on ourselves and our teams, depending on the size of the crowd. We haven't figured out that we're responsible for sowing the Word and God is responsible for the harvest. We need to resign from the position of general manager of the universe and let God do what only He can do. We can't generate a harvest, no matter how hard we try. Even when we're totally messed up, in His great grace, God blesses His Word and people are saved and grow in their faith.

A behavioral scientist studied aspiring leaders, and he observed a common phenomenon he termed "the arrival fallacy," which is the illusion that if we reach a cherished goal and finally get to our desired destination in our careers, we'll achieve lasting fulfillment. This isn't a rare condition. Our brains are wired to *want* even more than we enjoy *liking*, and we convince ourselves that lofty expectations will have a dramatic and long-term payoff.[21] It's a lie. I assumed I'd feel like the king of the mountain if Seacoast ever hit a number of people on a Sunday morning that I had previously thought unattainable. When that happened, it felt great . . . for a few minutes, and then I had an adrenaline crash the next day. By God's grace, we've hit many benchmarks, and with each one, I felt exhilarated, but only for a day or two. It's certainly not wrong to have goals and to pursue them, but we have misguided expectations if we think reaching them is what life is all about. If we reach them but miss out on loving, caring, supportive relationships, we've missed it all.

---

21 A.C. Shilton, "You Accomplished Something Great. So Now What?" *New York Times*, May 28, 2019, https://www.nytimes.com/2019/05/28/smarter-living/you-accomplished-something-great-so-now-what.html.

In training pastors, Tim Keller explains that there's always "a message under the message," and perceptive people in the audience will notice it. The subtexts are instantly recognizable to pastors, even to those who use them but don't want to admit it. Three of them are ways we look for approval from people, and the last one is true worship.

- "Don't you think I'm a great preacher?" We do everything possible to impress people, not with the gospel of grace, but with our expertise as communicators.
- "Don't you think our church is great?" We're on a constant PR campaign to make sure people are impressed with our churches.
- "Don't you think our programs are great?" We focus on our leadership pipeline, our discipleship programs, our community outreach, our children's ministry, and the other ways the church is making a difference.
- "Don't you think Christ is great?" We're deeply tapped into the wonder of grace for us, and God's love, power, and wisdom flow from us. As we preach, we're worshipping, which points people to God's greatness and goodness.[22]

It's ironic, isn't it? We have the most powerful, most fulfilling, most heart-warming message in the universe, but it's so incredibly easy to replace God's great love with poor substitutes. *Noticing* them is painful, *naming* them is essential, and *replacing*

---

22 Adapted from *Preaching* by Tim Keller (New York: Penguin Books, 2015), pp. 289-294.

them is the path to more joy and effectiveness than we ever dreamed possible.

It's human nature to compare, to see where we stand next to others who do what we do. It's interesting, though, that we invest our energies in comparison only in the areas where we might win or lose: Pastors compare themselves with other pastors, musicians compare themselves with other musicians, and engineers compare themselves with other engineers, writers with writers, athletes with athletes, and on and on. It's deeply ingrained in our nature . . . our fallen nature. In Psalm 73, the writer, Asaph, let comparison get the best of him. He looked around him, and he saw that other people, godless people, were advancing more than he was, made more money than he did, and were happier than he was. . . . and it really bothered him! He spends the first half of the psalm griping that life isn't fair, and by extension, God isn't fair. Then, he went into the sanctuary, and God gave him insight into the situation. This insight allowed him to gain a more secure footing—emotionally and spiritually. As Asaph reflects on how comparison affected him, he remembers: "Then I realized that my heart was bitter, and I was all torn up inside. I was so foolish and ignorant—I must have seemed like a senseless animal to you" (Psalm 73:21-22, NLT).

He had been so upset, so furious, that his emotions were out of control! Have you ever been in that dark place? I have, and I've met with countless pastors who can identify with Asaph. But when Asaph was at his worst, God didn't recoil, and He didn't blast him. Read Asaph's recollection:

Yet I still belong to you; you hold my right hand. You guide me with your counsel, leading me to a glorious destiny. Whom have I in heaven but you? I desire you more than anything on earth. My health may fail, and my spirit may grow weak, but God remains the strength of my heart; he is mine forever (vv. 23-26).

The remedy for idolatry, the antidote for comparison, is being ruthlessly honest with God. When we're at our worst, He reaches out in love and takes us by the hand. Nothing else will do.

When Asaph was at his worst, God reached out to take his hand. He assured the psalmist of His great love, tenderly leading him to truth, and reminding him that He ultimately makes all things right, even if we can't see it in the moment. Asaph's heart is melted by God's compassionate care. He exclaims that knowing God is far better than anything the heavens and the earth can offer, and in fact, "he is mine forever."

THE ENDURANCE FACTOR

The remedy for idolatry, the antidote for comparison, is being ruthlessly honest with God. When we're at our worst, He reaches out in love and takes us by the hand. Nothing else will do.

CHIP'S TAKE

Wow! Thank you, Pastor Greg, for honestly and vulnerably sharing your journey. I'd like to make a few observations as I've walked with you for over a decade now. As you've practiced and embraced the *experienced reality* of your heavenly Father's love on a daily basis, here's what I've noticed:

- You still care about what people think, but negative moments don't send you into as deep of a spiral, and you recover much more quickly.
- You're more present with people. You are really with the people you're with.
- I've noticed that you're less absorbed in what you think needs to happen in any given moment or encounter and how to make it happen. There's more of a sense of curiosity and anticipation than there is control.
- You seem more consistently at peace with your life and what's happening in it. You seem to be enjoying "the unforced rhythms of grace" Jesus promised.
- You navigated a critical season of transition that involved passing the baton of the leadership of Seacoast Church to your son, Josh. It would take another book to discuss what we've learned and continue to learn about the relational, emotional, and spiritual challenges that a leader

encounters when it's time to submit to God's gentle but firm promptings that this season of your life and leadership is over. You did it.

- You really care about younger leaders, their families, and their organizations. I believe this statement, "You can't be a father until you've been a son." I believe because you've allowed God to father you, you've learned to be a beloved son. That has enabled you to be a better father to your family and to the leaders God brings into your sphere of influence.

I haven't shared these things only to compliment Greg, although he does require a certain amount of that from us. I've shared these things to get you thinking about how a consistent experience of your heavenly Father's love might create positive changes in your life, relationships, and ministry. I would say without hesitation, it is the number one most important thing I've learned since becoming a Christian. I would also say the lack of a proper consistent experience of the Father's love is a major factor in many of the unhealthy habits, practices, and outcomes that leaders both create and experience.

I've worked with people who are struggling with every kind of sin, relational breakdown, mental and emotional health challenges, and plenty more, and I've learned some really cool stuff. I have come to believe that all of the dysfunctional cycles of thought, belief, and behavior that many of us struggle with are the result of *our attempts to meet a right need the wrong way.* It's not wrong to have needs. We all have needs. What gets us in trouble is going to the wrong source in the wrong way to get a right need met.

Is it wrong to need love? Is it wrong to need approval? Is it wrong to need encouragement? Is it wrong to need a sense of belonging and to be valued by others? Is it wrong to need intimacy? None of these things are wrong. The problem arises when we look to, run to, and rely on the wrong people and activities to meet those needs. Whoever or whatever we look to, run to, and rely on to meet those needs has power over us. Whether we intend to give that power away, or even realize we're giving it away, we are, in fact, giving away the power to control our thoughts, our emotions, and even our behavior.

> We all have needs. What gets us in trouble is going to the wrong source in the wrong way to get a right need met.

Some time ago, a pastor asked me to consult with him and his team. The first meeting was really positive, and the team was receptive to my ideas about orphans with cups and the fountain of living water. As the pastor walked me to my car in the late afternoon, he told me how blessed he felt to be doing what he'd always dreamed of doing in his leadership role in the church. He went into detail about the ways his gifts matched his role, but then he turned to me and asked, "But Chip, why am I not happy? Why can't I relax and enjoy what God has done? What's wrong with me?" These weren't rhetorical questions. He wanted answers.

At first I thought, "Sheesh, man. I've been pouring my heart out all day. I just want to go home and crash." But I realized this was a God-ordained moment, so I began asking some questions about his childhood and his relationship with his parents. At first, I think he wanted to give me the right answers, but in only a few minutes his defenses went down and he confided, "I never felt that I was good enough. I couldn't please them. No matter how well I did in school or sports, they always told me I could do better."

I told him, "That sounds pretty rough." I paused for a second and then asked, "How many dads do you have?"

He looked at me like a third eye had sprouted in my face, but then he got it. "You mean God?"

"Yeah, don't we call Him 'Father'?" I then asked, "Hey, do you want to fulfill God's purpose?" Before he said anything, I answered for him. "I know you do. You're what I call 'the real deal.' I'm just proud to be your friend." I paused again, and then I continued. "When we throw dirt on your casket, do you want people to say that this was a man who fulfilled God's purpose? He did what God created him to do."

He nodded, but he wasn't sure where this was going. I said, "If that's your goal, there's a really important question you need to answer: Why did God create you?"

Instantly, he went into his pastor mode: "To worship Him, to serve Him, to fulfill the Great Commission, to love Him with all my heart, soul, strength, and mind."

I shook my head and told him, "Stop all that nonsense! If God created us to worship Him, He's an egotistical rock star who wants people yelling His name. That doesn't work for me. If He created us to serve Him, it's like having children just to mow the grass and do the dishes." This wasn't a track he was familiar with, but he continued to listen. "Imagine the Trinity all by Himself, back before Genesis 1:1, before the creation of anything else—Father, Son, and Holy Spirit . . . and nothing else. What compelled Him to create the universe and the people on this planet?" He looked a bit confused, so I continued, "God didn't need us to worship Him or serve Him. He had plenty of angels for that." Why did He create you, me, and everyone else?

He was sure he had the answer now: "He created us to love Him."

"No, that's not it. Kind of close, but not quite there. That would be like Warren Buffett asking you to lunch and wanting you to pay for it. He doesn't need that! Why did God create you? Here's my answer and it's the only one that makes sense to me. *He created you so that He could love you.*" I let that settle for a minute, and then I pressed a bit more: "If that's correct, what's your purpose? It's this: *To recognize, receive, and rest in the Father's amazing love for you.* Everything else comes out of that, including your love for Him. Your task, then, is to allow God to pour His love into you so that it transforms you from the inside out."

I could tell his wheels were turning as he said, "You mean like John wrote in 1 John 4:19, 'We love, because He first loved us.'? My love for Him is a response to His love for me. I don't initiate it, He does."

"You got it. Worship, serving, evangelism, leadership . . . everything is a byproduct of our experience of God's great love, not a condition we meet to get Him to love us. We were created to live *from* love, not *for* love . . . *from an experience* of God's approval as His child, not *to earn* His approval by performance and rule-keeping . . . *from* the fulness of God's love, not *to get filled* by using people and things."

A lot of Christians, including church leaders, make the mistake of making the consequences of receiving God's love into conditions for deserving His love. We will never be able to earn or deserve God's love. It's a gift and working to deserve it not only tires us out—it also dishonors the giver of the gift. In other words, we substitute sanctification for justification, trusting our growth, devotional life, and service to please God, when we're already totally forgiven by Christ's sacrifice on the cross and counted as righteous because His perfect life is credited to our account. When we get that backward, we unplug our hearts from the only source of love, joy, peace, and power. When I teach this concept, some people think they've got me cornered.

They'll say, "You're teaching cheap grace." My response is that there's nothing cheap about it. There was an infinite price paid, but not by us. Someone else paid it for us.

Sometimes I'm asked, "Yeah, but what about John 14:15, where Jesus said, 'If you love Me, you will keep my commandments'?" I respond. "Think about it. John also wrote, 'We love, because He first loved us.' It goes like this: When we experience the magnificent, soul-nourishing love of God, we naturally love Him in return, and we want to honor those we love. So the order is important: It's not 'obey to be loved;' it's 'experience God's love, love Him back, and let that love overflow into glad obedience to whatever He wants you to do.'" At that point, I often point them to another verse in John's first letter: "We have come to know and have believed the love which God has for us. God is love, and the one who remains in love remains in God, and God remains in him" (1 John 4:16). Our lives are transformed when we "come to know" and "believe" the love God pours out to us. It's criminal that so many preachers, teachers, and leaders get that backward, insisting that God's love is contingent on our loving Him first and our obedience. A lot of problems in the church come from that rotten root.

On the cross, love and justice come together. God is a just judge, so He has to punish sin. He could have let us bear the punishment of eternal destruction and isolation, but instead, Jesus took our place and paid for it all. His last word was "Tetelstai," which means "It is finished," or "paid in full." Why did Jesus take on the hell we deserve? Love. That's it. Just love. No cheap grace there. It's very expensive, but we didn't have to pay it.

When I talk to staff teams or speak at conferences about the love of God, there is often a holy silence with some muffled weeping. Plenty of people have told me later that this teaching about God's love revolutionized their lives. I don't doubt it. That's what it did for me!

We're right to put a lot of emphasis on Jesus—His life, death, resurrection, and ascension—and we often give plenty of space to talk about the Spirit's work in and through us. Nothing at all wrong with that, but I'm afraid we often leave someone out— the Father. In one of Jesus' most famous statements, He said, "I am the way, and the truth, and the life; no one comes to the Father except through me" (John 14:6). Something wonderful happens when we meet and develop our relationship with Jesus; something else wonderful happens when we meet and develop our relationship with the Holy Spirit, but something even more wonderful, something even deeper, happens when we meet and develop our relationship with The Father.

Jesus taught us to pray, "Our Father . . ." Some people make a sharp distinction between the Father and Jesus. They see the God of the Old Testament as harsh and demanding, and they see Jesus as tender and kind. Jesus told us that, if you've seen Me, you've seen The Father, and that He only said and did what He saw and heard The Father saying and doing. In other words, as the writer to the Hebrews reminds us:

THE ENDURANCE FACTOR

> God, after He spoke long ago to the fathers in the prophets in many portions and in many ways, in these last days has spoken to us in His Son, whom He appointed heir of all things, through whom He also made the world. And He is the radiance of His glory and the exact representation of His nature, and upholds all things by the word of His power. When He had made purification of sins, He sat down at the right hand of the Majesty on high. —Hebrews 1:1-3, author emphasis

So, what's going on here? Why are we talking so much about the Father's love? There's nothing wrong with a desire to be effective, to be respected, and to have a measure of influence and authority . . . as long as those desires are second (or third or fourth) to our desire to experience the love of God. It's an issue of priority, not right and wrong. Jeremiah quotes God as He shared His heart:

> This is what the Lord says: 'Let no wise man boast of his wisdom, nor let the mighty man boast of his might, nor a rich man boast of his riches; but let the one who boasts boast of this, that he understands and knows Me, that I am the LORD who exercises mercy, justice, and righteousness on the earth; for I delight in these things,' declares the LORD. —Jeremiah 9:23-24

A "boast" is what we depend on, the object of our hope, the source of our identity, worth, and value. We boast in the areas we want to be known for. There's nothing in the world wrong with being smart, powerful, or rich (to name just three common pursuits), as long as these aren't our boast. When God, the mighty Creator, Savior, and Friend is our boast, our deepest desire is to "understand and know" Him. When that's our heart's desire, we'll find Him to be amazingly merciful, just, and free from any manipulative motives.

Jesus talked about thirst and two sources of water in John 4. Jesus blew through all social and religious conventions to talk with the Samaritan woman, who had multiple marriages and was living in sin at the time, when He met her by a well. Their conversation was all about quenching thirst from the right source. Jesus began by asking her for a drink of water. She was astounded that a Jewish man would stoop to converse with a Samaritan woman—and what if He knew the whole truth about her? I can almost see Jesus chuckle as He told her, "If you knew the gift of God, and who it is who is saying to you, 'Give Me a drink,' you would have asked Him, and He would have given you living water" (John 4:10). Of course, she didn't get it. She tried to figure it out, but Jesus then gave her a staggering promise: "Everyone who drinks of this water *[I imagine Him pointing to the well.]* will be thirsty again; but whoever drinks of the water that I will give him *shall never be thirsty;* but the water that I will give him will become *in him* a fountain of water springing up to eternal life" (vv. 13-14, *author emphasis*). Christian philosopher Dallas Willard defined spiritual thirst as "the pain or discomfort of unmet need." We can try to meet our needs *from the outside in* by running after physical, visible, tangible things like success, influence, and pleasure, but as Jesus told the woman, we'll only be thirsty again. Those things are wonderful, but only if they're secondary. When we make them primary, they're poison to our souls. They simply can't and won't ever quench our thirst. But Jesus offered the woman, and He offers us, a different kind of water—not a stagnant well, but a fountain springing up to eternal life from within us. This kind satisfies us from the inside out; it meets our deepest needs, and because it's a fountain on the inside, it keeps on meeting them.

> **If you learn to go to God first and most, your deep thirst will be quenched, and you won't look over your shoulder all day to see if anyone is getting ahead of you.**

When you wake up each morning, if your checklist that determines if you're okay is outside in—how many, how much, who likes me, who doesn't, what are the latest posts on my social media account—you have two problems: you're boasting in externals, and you're going to remain thirsty. But if you learn to go to God first and most, your deep thirst will be quenched, and you won't look over your shoulder all day to see if anyone is getting ahead of you.

The good news is that the fountain is portable. We can take it with us to the boardroom and the bedroom, to staff meetings and the pulpit, when we're washing the car or caring for the poor. All day every day, we can drink deeply of the fountain of His love.

My goal since I've learned this is to walk into every room not needing anything from anyone in that room. My inner narrative has become second nature: "God, *I want* these people to like me, *I want* to do a good job, and *I want* You to use me in their lives, *but I don't need* these things to know that You're love is supremely important and I'm okay without them." It's the same in my relationship with Coleen, our kids, Greg, our team, our neighbors, and every other person in my world—*I want* them to love me, like me, and think I'm the greatest thing since the designated hitter rule, but because my heart is filled and overflowing with the epignosis, or experienced reality, of God's love, *I don't need* them to feel that way about me. In fact, I found that the secret of a great marriage is to have an affair . . . a love affair with God. It's a lot more pure and delightful love when a couple comes together without needing each other to be okay. If they need each other's affection to be okay, they're like *two ticks and no dog*—not very satisfying (except for the dog). They're trying to get something from each other that neither of them has. As

THE ENDURANCE FACTOR

I've said before, when two people encounter each other *from fullness* rather than *for* fullness, they can love without manipulating, posing, or playing games to get the love they crave and avoid being hurt again.

I've talked to pastors who have built large, successful ministries, but they're not happy or fulfilled. The place they've attained has not quenched their deep, inner thirst. No matter how successful they are, it's not enough. In the next chapter, we'll talk about four Meta-Skills that will create a "Guard-Your-Heart Toolbox" to equip and empower you to LIVE WELL and FINISH STRONG in every area of life.

CHAPTER 6

THE LONG ROAD BACK

GREG'S TAKE

I remember when one of our Seacoast staff members, Mack Lake, invited Chip to meet with him and the rest of the team to help us make progress in working together. (We mentioned this in chapter one.) For some reason, Mack scheduled thirty-minute appointments for each of us to meet individually with Chip. I wasn't looking forward to my slot. I had no idea what we'd talk about. I was fine. I didn't need any help, but I dutifully walked into the room and sat down with him at my appointed time. In only a few minutes, Chip knew more about me than I knew about myself! I found myself telling him how my concept of God had been shaped by my family and my past church experiences, and one of my primary motivations was to do enough so God wasn't angry (or at least disappointed) with me. Chip patiently and persistently explained that my view of God was way off target, and in fact, God is delighted that I'm His child! It was a monumental U-turn for me, and in all the years I've known him, Chip has only reinforced and deepened my understanding of God's amazing love, so I can relax in His warm, strong love.

The change has been remarkable. Thanks to Chip, I began to see that I had been living and ministering to gain approval, not from my secure position of already having God's approval. I lived with a shaky identity—never quite good enough, and tired of trying to measure up. I was well aware that I missed God's mark in countless ways all day every day, and I couldn't imagine Him ever really smiling when He thought of me. I intuitively (and incorrectly) believed that if I pleased and impressed people, their approval would fill the hole in my soul, and if I worked really hard to build a great church, surely that would earn some points with God. (Some of you may be thinking, *What in the world is wrong with that guy? Doesn't he know the gospel?* And others of you are thinking, *I know exactly what's wrong with that guy because I feel the same way!*) If I could give people a picture of my view of God for most of my life, it's the last combat scene in *Saving Private Ryan*. Captain Miller had led his squad through the French countryside after D-Day to find Private Ryan and bring him home because his three brothers had been killed, and the Army didn't want all four of them to die.

The squad lost several men in the search, and when they found Ryan, he didn't want to leave his buddies who were in the thick of the fight with the Germans. In a bloody siege on a bridge, Miller was shot. As he was dying, he pulled Ryan close and told him in a raspy, weak voice, "Earn this. Earn it." Years later, the film shows Ryan, now an old man, visiting the American cemetery in Normandy where thousands of brave Americans are buried. As he knelt next to Captain Miller's headstone, he weeps and tells his wife, "Tell me I'm a good man." In other words, "Tell me I've earned it."[23] That's how I felt day after day after day: *Somebody please tell me I'm a good man! Tell me I've earned respect. Tell me you approve of me!*

> **The Father's affirmation of you and me is apart from our performance. He loves us simply because we belong to Him.**

I've had to think, memorize, meditate, and talk about the wonder of God's love because it's so different from what I'd imagined for most of my life. I often need to remind myself that if I'm

---

23 Spielberg, Steven. 1998. *Saving Private Ryan*. United States: DreamWorks Distribution.

THE ENDURANCE FACTOR

"in Christ," the Father's view of Jesus is the same as His view of me. So when the voice came from heaven at Jesus' baptism, "This is my beloved Son, with whom I am well pleased," He's saying that to me, too. At the Jordan that day, Jesus hadn't done anything in ministry, so the Father wasn't announcing that Jesus had earned His affirmation. It was totally apart from His performance. And the Father's affirmation of you and me is apart from our performance too. He loves us simply because we belong to Him.

This doesn't mean all of my ministry before this revelation was invalid. God used me as a willing vessel to communicate the gospel of grace, and lives were changed. Sadly, though, I wasn't experiencing that grace as much as God wanted me to. I've had to dig deep into the truth of God's Word to understand my identity as God's beloved child—which is the foundation of my security and peace. In chapter two, I mentioned the concept of being created in the image of God. Here, I want to expand on this life-changing truth: The opening pages of Genesis tell us that we were created in God's image. Animals, plants, mountains, rocks, and seas don't have that distinction, only human beings. We are the crown jewel of His creation! What does that mean? It doesn't mean we're exactly like Him. We can't approach his noncommunicable traits, such as omnipresence, omniscience, omnipotence, immutability, and self-existence. But He has imparted to us the capacity to experience and express His love, goodness, and kindness.

Since the Holy Spirit used Chip to open my eyes to the wonder and life-changing power of the Father's love, I've had the privilege of paying it forward wherever I go . . . including in the pages of this book. In the ancient world, images of kings were erected as statues, carved on buildings, or stamped on coins to let people know his rule extended wherever his image could be seen. The principle is true of us too: We're created in God's image, and when people see us representing the King of all, they know His reign extends everywhere we live, love, and serve.

But in the story of mankind, it didn't take long for things to go off the rails. The long arc of the Scripture is creation, fall, redemption, and restoration in the new heavens and new earth. The first two, creation and fall, are seen in the first three chapters of Genesis, redemption takes most of the rest of the Bible, and the new heavens and new earth are predicted from time to time in the Old and New Testaments but the fulfillment is described at the end of Revelation. Sin didn't completely obliterate the image of God in us, but it certainly disfigured it. Instead of moral purity, immoral behavior became the default mode of the human heart, our intellect is corrupted by lies and misunderstanding, our speech often does more harm than good, and our relationships are clouded by selfishness instead of love. The gospel is God's solution. The Old Testament pointed forward to a day when an ultimate sacrifice or sin would take the place of sheep, goats, and bulls, and when the perfect sacrifice was made, God would change hearts of stone into hearts of flesh—tender, receptive, and alive. That day happened outside the walls of Jerusalem almost two millennia ago.

Today, we have the incredible honor and responsibility to represent God in everything we think, say, and do. We're beneficiaries of God's grace, and He calls us to be His agents and His ambassadors to extend His loving reign. Paul captured the heart and purpose of living as God's representatives this way: "Imitate God, therefore, in everything you do, because you are his dear children. Live a life filled with love, following the example of Christ. He loved us and offered himself as a sacrifice for us, a pleasing aroma to God" (Ephesians 5:1-2, NLT).

If you've got a pulse, God has a plan.

I've talked to pastors who have beautifully taught the truth of being made in the image of God, but they don't feel it, they don't live it, and at the bottom of their hearts, they don't believe it's true of them. They may be filled with shame because of something they've done. They may look at the success of others and assume they're insignificant and disposable. They may feel crushed under the strain of leading obstinate people. They may believe that opportunities have passed them by, and they see only a bleak future. I have good news: If you've got a pulse, God has a plan.

As co-rulers with God, we follow Jesus' example. After James and John jockeyed for the prime positions in the cabinet they expected Jesus to form when He took the throne over Israel, Jesus set them (and the other disciples and us) straight:

> You know that the rulers of the Gentiles domineer over them, and those in high position exercise authority over them. It is not this way among you, but whoever wants to become prominent among you shall be your servant, and whoever desires to be first among you shall be your slave; just as the Son of Man did not come to be served, but to serve, and to give His life as a ransom for many. —Matthew 20:25-28

The long road back may begin, and it regularly includes, a refresher course about our identity as God's beloved children and our privilege to represent Him to everyone around us. Our identity is the unchanging bedrock of our confidence, our calling is to be God's responsive children, ambassadors, and servants in everything we do, and our assignment is our current place and role where we act as God's agents. One more thing: our sins, doubts, and struggles don't nullify God's purpose for us. Adam and Eve still had the same purpose of representing God as image-bearers, but their sin just made it harder. We have two things they didn't have: overwhelming forgiveness through the grace of Jesus Christ . . . and the indwelling presence of the Holy Spirit to comfort, guide, empower, and change us from the inside out. As we get more in touch with our purpose of bearing the image of God, we can tap into His limitless resources. After Jesus met with the Samaritan woman at Jacob's well, she was so excited to have met the Messiah that she ran into town to tell everyone about Him. At the same time, the disciples were coming back with lunch. They encouraged him to eat, but He told them, "I have food to eat that you do not know about." The disciples were, as usual, confused by Jesus' answer, so He explained, "My food is to do the will of Him who sent Me, and to accomplish His work" (John 4:32, 34).

Are you eating the food of performance . . . or comparison . . . or hopelessness . . . or resentment and self-pity? These things promise to satisfy us, but they can't, they don't, and they never will. Eat the food of God's pardon, presence, purpose, and power . . . and be filled to overflowing.

I have the tremendous joy to create retreat environments where leaders feel safe enough to pour out their hearts and experience understanding from one another and the love of the Father. When a pastor I'll call Philip came, I wasn't sure if he needed a retreat or the hospital. He was so broken, so emotionally shattered that he physically shook. He explained that his wife had left him, his children wouldn't speak to him, and while he was at the retreat, his church board was considering replacing him. And he was deeply in debt. Over the course of the days Philip was with us, he remarked over and over again that he hadn't felt such love and support ever—not just lately, but ever. He was a sponge, soaking in the theology of being a beloved child of God and relishing the encouragement of the other men in the group. As the men left on the last day, I was sure God had done some remarkable things, but I wasn't sure how remarkable. A few months later, Philip called to tell me that God had given him such stability and security that he could be honest with his wife, his grown kids, and the board at the church about his fears and his pattern of avoidance to minimize conflict. God's great love had given him the strength to confess to each one, and he was learning to live out his new identity by taking responsibility for every interaction. No more hiding, no more running, no more lying . . . to others or to himself. Philip was a changed man.

An older man I'll call Richard had served for years as an assistant pastor. He came to the retreat because he was devastated by his wife's recent death. His grief was compounded by the fact that the church had hired a new, young pastor, who didn't seem to appreciate Richard's gentle, patient ministry to people in the congregation. On the first day he was with us, he couldn't stop weeping. He told us, "My whole life is in shambles! I don't know how to cope with it all." He explained, "If I'm fired, there aren't many churches looking for a sixty-five-year-old assistant pastor whose primary calling is to care for the elderly of the church." He told us that he had spent all his money on his wife's treatment for cancer, and he had no cushion at all. He missed a breakfast or two because he desperately needed to sleep, but when he was with us, he was all there. About four months after the retreat, he wrote me a letter to let me know that the love he felt at the retreat had given him a renewed sense of stability and hope. He was still employed, and he was using what he learned in his time with us to encourage those in his care.

THE ENDURANCE FACTOR

Let some of the people who have come to our retreats weigh in on the stresses and strains they felt before they arrived and how they were refreshed so they could endure and thrive:

Jason Brinkley

As a husband, father of four, and the pastor of a growing church, there is never a time when I don't have to be "on." I'm always in one of those four roles, and each has its own very real weight and list of ongoing responsibilities. Though I love my wife, kids, and church, the constant pressure to be present and engaged takes its toll. The Retreat at Church Creek gave me a chance to just be me. Three days with nothing to do but rest and recharge with a band of brothers who all share the same struggles and feel the same pressures. It was so encouraging to hear how similar our struggles were, even though our contexts were all different.

The transparent and authentic conversations were refreshing, and I left with a few connections that have provided me with friends I can lean on for ongoing encouragement and connection.

Being at the retreat had an ongoing impact on my life and ministry in two ways. First, it helped me see how important it is for me to take a few days to myself each year. I do a pretty good job of managing my own soul and overall health. With that being said, I have not taken extended time away by myself. I really saw the benefit of doing that at the retreat, especially doing it with other pastors. The other big thing being at the retreat did for me was give me a greater desire to serve and encourage other pastors. Heading into the "second half" of my life this year, I feel I can be of some encouragement and support for younger pastors in my own community and network.

Cliff Branam

Over the past nine years, I've been pioneering restorative services for the poor in Central Appalachia. While it's extremely rewarding work, it's taken a toll on me. Pre-retreat, I had passed the point of exhaustion and was years into burnout. I was contemplating the future of ministry, and it didn't look promising. However, God created an opportunity for me to visit The Retreat at Church Creek, and I am so thankful He did. The retreat was on the frontend of a twenty-eight-day extended break. On my first morning walk around the property, I encountered the Father's embrace. The Holy Spirit comforted me as only He can and breathed life into me spiritually and relationally.

I made several new friends throughout the retreat, and God provided an amazing mentor that is now a cherished friend. This was my answer to prayer. I now keep a picture in my office to remind me of the exact spot at the retreat where the Holy Spirit met me that day. It was like leaving the battlefield believing I was maimed but realizing I was only dehydrated.

I thank God for my time at the retreat. It was truly an answer to prayer.

Upon return, I was back in the trenches. I immediately had to terminate a clinical physiologist who was vital to our mission. In addition, I had to face the death of a man residing in one of our transitional homes. As difficult as these circumstances were, I was prepared. My time at the retreat was instrumental in giving me strength, wisdom, and hope.

John Dowdey

I realized I was dangerously tired. In that state of fatigue, I found myself doubting what God called me to do. I began to question if I truly had what it takes to lead effectively. I found myself alone, isolated, tired, and frustrated. That's when an invite to Retreat at Church Creek was extended at an ARC Conference. Fighting my own insecurities, self-doubt, and fears, I signed up and went. There, I found what was missing . . . rest and meaningful relationships. Sitting around a table with men I did not know before the trip, a bond was formed. I found a place where I could let my guard down and lean into other pastors who experienced much of the same struggles as me. Watching the sunrise, listening to the birds, and riding on the boat, I realized God created a space for me to stop, rest, delight, and worship Him. The best gift I can give my wife, my family, my church, and my community is a healthy me. I would not have discovered this without the opportunity to rest at Church Creek. I met lifelong friends at that table, and we committed to each other to finish strong!

Coming back home from such an incredible experience had its challenges. The enemy doesn't like it when we discover healthy rhythms in leadership; he wants us as tired and defeated as possible. It was no surprise I came home to heavy decisions. When I left the Retreat at Church Creek, I made a commitment to live well and to not do ministry alone. Instead of settling for self-talk that was negative and defeating, I called a friend I met at the Church Creek. He reminded me of my purpose and calling and simply said, "You have what it takes."

Paul Cooper

I can't tell you the reason why I wanted to go to the Retreat at Church Creek, but I can tell you that God knew I needed to be there. I received the invitation from one of the retreat sponsors. I felt like others could use the retreat more than me, so I passed the information along to a few other pastors. Each time they said they could not attend, the sponsor told me, "Maybe you should go." Finally (I'm a little slow), I got the hint that Holy Spirit wanted me to go, so I registered.

Fast forward a few months: Hurricane Irma hit our area of central Florida. I was knee deep (literally) in the middle of hurricane cleanup when it was time to go to Church Creek. Again, I made excuses that I could not attend. On a return trip from a hurricane outreach, my boss asked when I was leaving. I told him I was not going to go because of all the work overseeing with the hurricane cleanup. He wisely told me I need to go. He said, "The cleanup will still be here when you get back." Still, I was not going to go, but my wife said I needed to go. Okay, God, I get it. I'll go! And boy, am I glad I did!

What an amazing few days of relaxing, being refreshed, and building relationships. I had no idea how much I needed this time until I was in the midst of being there. By the end, I felt recharged and ready to attack some issues that had been building up over the years. Thank you so much, Pastor Greg and the Retreat at Church Creek!

Do you feel like things can never be good again? Are you afraid you've passed the point of no return? Are you hanging on by your fingernails, and you're not sure how long you can last? In countless conversations with pastors over the decades, and especially in the past few years, I've learned that security, confidence, and hope are elusive for many church leaders. I urge you, I plead with you, don't give up! Dive deeper into the Scriptures that proclaim the message of God's limitless love, forgiveness, and grace, and find at least one person who will cheer you on as you take each step toward wholeness.

CHIP'S TAKE

I love hearing the stories of what God does at The Retreat at Church Creek. It's so exciting and rewarding to hear how the lives of leaders are impacted by an intentional environment of grace, truth, and time. I discovered years ago through reading Dr. Henry Cloud and Dr. John Townsend that those last three words are the ingredients necessary to create an environment that nourishes and supports growth and change.

GRACE	TRUTH	TIME
Grace says, "I love and accept you just the way you are."	Truth says, "But I love you too much to leave you the way you are."	Times says, "You didn't get this way in a day. And I will walk beside you for as long as it takes, without judgment."
Grace believes everyone is doing the best they can with what they have.	Truth is not looking to assign fault or blame. It's about recognizing and breaking the cycle of cause and effect, "Root and Fruit".	Time recognizes that change is a process, not an event.

When we learn to create and inhabit environments that maintain a balance of tension between these three ingredients, we're able to invite others into the courageous journey of recognizing their destructive patterns of thought, belief, and behavior, and we can partner with God to change them.

THE ENDURANCE FACTOR

Pastor Greg and the team at The Retreat at Church Creek do a great job of creating this environment. You can observe men and women who attend the retreats slowly find rest, encouragement, and rejuvenating interaction with other people just like themselves. For decades, I've spent a lot of time thinking about how we can build and maintain a life of intimacy and impact, passion, and purpose. What set of habits, practices, commitments, and relationships will empower and support my desire to live well and finish strong in every area of my life? How do we develop a sustainable and effective way to experience grace, truth, and time in a healthy environment in our everyday lives? I've spent a lot of time thinking about this and experimenting with what works and what doesn't. In this chapter I want to share my current toolbox of practices and commitments that I believe will serve you very well in your pursuit of an amazing life.

Please, may I take just another minute to provoke and motivate you? Jesus said in John 10:10, "The thief comes only to steal and kill and destroy. I came so that they would have life, and have it abundantly." I have come to believe that the enemy's greatest act of theft isn't from what you currently have. His greatest act of theft is *keeping you from getting what God wants you to have.* In this chapter, I'm going to address some things you may already know. *Knowing* them doesn't change your life, but doing them until they become "embodied truth" in your life certainly will. They literally become a part of your everyday existence to nourish and empower you to live a life beyond "what you could ask or even imagine" (Ephesians 3:20, author paraphrase). Can I push you just a tad more? If you don't do anything different between now and next year, don't whine when you realize your life hasn't gotten any better. Do something about it! There are tools available to us that really, really work, but we have to work them. Not all at once. Not perfectly from the start. But we have to start.

Do you know there was a time you couldn't touch your finger to your nose? When you were a baby, your arms flailed around you without any conscious control. Eventually, you learned that you could direct them where you want them to go. Then you were able to do it seemingly without thinking. Your brain, nervous system, and muscles learned, practiced, and stored the information necessary to move your arms where you wanted them to go. You can do the same thing with the cultivation, renovation, and development of the habits and practices that will make you healthier and stronger from the inside out, in fact, healthier than you've ever been before. Let's talk about what we'll call the "Live Well–Finish Strong Toolbox." It's a set of skills or meta-skills that enable you to identify, challenge, and change your destructive patterns of thought, belief, and behavior that continue to sabotage your pursuit of the life you want and that God wants for you.

These skills may or may not be part of your normal life rhythms, but they can become "embodied truths"—new habits formed by repetition and intensity. In physical activity, like walking, typing, or playing a sport, we begin by making laborious efforts, but with regular practice, the actions become more natural and fluid. That's the nature of embodied truths.

Practice makes possible. It taps into the mysterious process by which what is difficult at first becomes progressively easier and more pleasurable—like learning to play tennis or the guitar. As we practice, our brains are developing new neural pathways connected to our muscles, so we learn to make these movements unconsciously. We often call this "muscle memory." The principle also operates in other aspects of life, like speaking the truth and setting reasonable boundaries in relationships, eating a healthy diet, regular exercise, and spiritual disciplines. In other words, if you want to develop a habit, any habit, you need to find ways to repeat it and connect emotionally with the action. Earlier in the book, we saw that we were imprinted by wonderful or terrible experiences, especially in childhood but throughout our lives. Developing better habits is creating new, positive imprints that have a powerful effect on us even when we're not consciously aware of them.

How do people change? And why don't more people experience real freedom and lasting change? In the body of Christ, we have an "information fixation." We believe that acquiring the right information results in life transformation. This assumption is profoundly wrong! It's one of the main reasons (I'd argue it's *the* main reason) we teach and teach and teach, but we aren't producing disciples who look much like Jesus. Their heads are full, but their hearts haven't been sufficiently moved. Adding new information to people's minds doesn't automatically uproot, overthrow, and defeat what's already there. Here's an interesting perspective from Jeremiah 1:10 (NIV, *author emphasis*): "See, today I appoint you over nations and kingdoms to uproot and tear down, to destroy and overthrow, to build and to plant."

In a single verse, we find six things that are the result of his ministry—to uproot, tear down, destroy, overthrow, and to build and plant. Four of the six, or two-thirds, are destructive. Two of the six, or one-third, are constructive. As I've watched and worked with people over four decades, I believe this is the perfect picture of spiritual growth. Two-thirds of spiritual growth is about getting rid of unhealthy and unhelpful stuff that's already there, and one-third is putting new stuff in. Remember when we talked about the parable of the sower in Mark 4 earlier in the book? Our hearts have pre-existing conditions based on our experiences up to this point in our lives, and these determine how the Word that we hear makes progress in our hearts and bears the fruit of Christlikeness.

The deeper change happens in us, the wider our impact on the people around us. If you're known for being caustic and snarky, it's not enough to address this problem on the surface and grit your teeth, saying, "I'll be nice today." No, you have to dig deep into your heart to uncover the painful imprints created by past hurts. Then you'll begin to connect the dots and realize your cynicism is a defense mechanism to keep people from getting too close (or whatever else it might be). As you invite the Father to love you at your deepest place and heal your deepest hurts, you'll be more secure, less defensive, less cynical, and the love of Jesus will overflow more than you ever imagined.

> # The deeper change happens in us, the wider our impact on the people around us.

As I talk to people who keep doing the same things and expecting different results, I want to say, "C'mon, people. We're smarter than this!" If you want to live well and finish strong, you need to develop a set of practices that do both the destructive and the constructive work God wants to do in your heart and life. If you don't, the negative imprints will continue to be the operating system of your life, and you'll repeat your problems everywhere you go and in every season in your future. We could examine dozens of skills and habits, but I focus on four practiced, tested, proven spiritual tools or meta-skills. If these become woven into the fabric of your life, you'll be far more resilient, far more compassionate, far happier, and far more effective. No, I'm not overstating it. I believe that promise with all my heart. I teach these in depth in our Leadership Huddles but let me give a thumbnail sketch of them now.

#1: Find Your "Band of Brothers or Sisters."

Find a small group of your peers with whom you can truly be yourself. Remember Genesis 3:10 and 2:25? After the Fall in Genesis 3 (author paraphrase), Adam and Eve were "afraid because they were naked, so they hid." They believed that their flaws made them unattractive and unable to be welcomed into God's presence. They lost what they had in Genesis 2:25 (NIV) before the fall—"they were both naked and felt no shame." They were fully known and fully loved. That's what we're all looking for, and until we find it, we live posing and pretending that we're something we're not. We expend a remarkable amount of energy attempting to be what we think other people want us to be. We all need to find a "tribe," a small group of people who know us, the good, the bad, and the ugly parts and still love us. The other thing we need in our tribe is people who will speak the truth to us when we need it.

Find your tribe or build one. Make a commitment to go deeper than surface and shop. Learn to listen to one another's story. Do the work to create a "masks off" community—being authentic and honest with each other and allowing others to speak into our lives.

How often do you connect with these people? I think once a month can work if the commitment and consistency is high. Reflect on what an environment of grace, truth, and time would look like. Discuss it with your tribe. Then walk toward it.

#2: Develop a Conversational Relationship with God Through Journaling.

God is the best friend, best counselor, and best leader in the universe. He knows us far better than we know ourselves, and He demonstrated His affection for us on the cross. Remember our discussion about "I see stuck people"? God wants to fellowship with you and reveal to you the deeper issues that are keeping you stuck in repeating, self-sabotaging cycles. His best work is always from the inside out. Whenever you're stuck, look inside with God's help and guidance. I have found and practiced for over thirty years that journaling with an expectation that God will meet with you there is an amazing way to develop our relationship with Him, and the practice also gives Him the opportunity to speak into our lives to bring about growth and change.

Many leaders use a journal to help them focus during their devotional times with God. I'm a big advocate. Writing slows you down, it makes you put your thoughts together, and it puts your ideas into coherent streams. Writing invites God into the process, because when you slow down enough to journal, He sneaks in to give insight and wisdom you wouldn't have noticed otherwise. Gregory Boyd wrote a wonderful book called *Seeing Is Believing: Experiencing Jesus through Imaginative Prayer*.[24] He encourages readers to put themselves in scenes in the Bible and imagine Jesus stepping into our situations with that beautiful and powerful blend of grace and truth.

---

24 Boyd, G. A. (2004). *Seeing Is Believing: Experience Jesus Through Imaginative Prayer*. Baker Books.

Here's a quick taste of a way you can invite God into your journal. Join me in the following exercise:

Find a quiet spot away from others so nobody can see what you're writing. Get quiet on the inside and outside. Slow down, take your time, and follow these four prompts:

1) Make a list of what you like about God. I'm not talking about the characteristics described in systematic theology. How would you describe Him as a person, a friend, an acquaintance?

2) Make a list of what you like about yourself.

3) Write God an email and tell Him what you like about Him. Be descriptive. Give examples.

4) Ask God what He likes about you. Write whatever comes to mind. You can throw it away later, but as you listen, trust that He has something to say to you.

Almost always when I've done this in a group, at least a few people wipe tears away as they write the last part. I then tell them, "Find one other person and share anything you want to share from this exercise. Don't share anything you don't want to. It's your call." I give them some time for this. Again, more tears. And then I bring the team back together and ask, "Does anyone want to share what the exercise meant to you?" No pressure at all, but usually, more than one person wants to talk about what God said to them. It's very common for people to feel like God snuck into the exercise and spoke to them. The cool thing is—He's always nicer to us than we are to ourselves.

Journaling maximizes reflection. When we write our prayers and God's answers, we increasingly sense His presence. The more we practice opening our hearts and minds to Him, the more we'll hear as He speaks to us. Rest in God's goodness at the moment. You can test what you write later. Doubt blocks the flow.

> **Journaling maximizes reflection. When we write our prayers and God's answers, we increasingly sense His presence.**

#3: Learn to Go to God First and Most for Everything You Need.

Many of us start our days with a cup of coffee and an open Bible. We sip and read, and we spend some time praying over our concerns. That's great, but what if during that time we stopped, opened our hands to God in a physical demonstration of submission and helplessness, and prayed, "Father, I'm not here to get anything done. I'm just here to receive more of Your love. This is why You created me. This is why I exist." Remember the Mac Lake story in chapter five? If you really want to fulfill God's greatest desire and your greatest assignment you need to make it a daily practice to let God love. Start your day allowing Him to speak your name and say over you, "This is my son/daughter whom I love dearly, and I'm very pleased with him/her." Soak in that love and affirmation. Carry it with you into your day. Sit quietly for five minutes or more to let the Father's love flow over you and into you. He might use a passage of Scripture, a song, an impression, or some other image or experience. Don't hurry. This is the most important time of your day. It's also a good time to remind yourself, "This is going to be a great day because I have a Father who adores me and has a wonderful plan for my life!"

#4: Detox Your Soul by Killing Your ANTs.

One of the most helpful skills you can develop is "thought awareness." Most of us seldom, if ever, stop and analyze what's going on in our thought lives. A toxic thought jumps into our minds, probably from a painful imprint from years before, but it's so familiar to us that we don't grab it and challenge it. We call these "Automatic Negative Thoughts," or ANTs. They sound like this:

"I'm such a stupid fool!"

"I can't do anything right!"

"I can't afford to fail, or else."

"I can't afford to be wrong, or I'll look foolish."

"I have to exceed others' expectations to feel good about myself."

"I can't let people know what's really going on with me, or they'll leave me or make fun of me."

"I have to always be on guard to protect myself."

THE ENDURANCE FACTOR

"I'm worthless, flawed, and unlovable."

"I'm not as smart as, not as handsome as, not as gifted as . . ."

Do you recognize anything like that going on in your mind sometimes? Even fairly often? Especially when you've failed or someone disapproves of you? Join the club.

Far too often, toxic ANTs are so normalized that we just stew in them until we find something to distract us from the pain they inflict again and again. We can "detox our souls" by recognizing the thoughts, grabbing them, and replacing them with God's loving truths. Yes, it's helpful to go back to the source that formed the painful imprints, but it's just as important to "take every thought captive to the obedience of Christ" and "destroy" the ANTs with the power of truth, our identity as beloved children of the King, and masterpieces in His eyes (2 Corinthians 10:3-5; Ephesians 2:10). To make this easy to remember, follow this three-step flow: capture, question, and replace.

1) *Capture* the thought. Write it down.

2) *Question* it. Ask it the following questions: Who told you that? Is it true? Would my spouse or friends agree with it? What was the trigger (a conversation, a failure, a snub, or whatever) that caused it? What past painful event (or events) produced the imprint that created the trigger?

3) *Replace* the ANT with an affirming truth from the Scriptures. Memorize it, let it sink deep into your soul, and use it quickly (or as quickly as you first capture and question an ANT).

As we learn to embody the four meta-skills, we experience "the peace of God that surpasses all understanding" (Philippians 4:7, author paraphrase), not distracted or discouraged by ANTs. We're all familiar with Jesus' invitation to rest in Matthew 11, but few of us experience it. This kind of rest isn't laying in a hammock watching the world go by. It's an inner connection with the One who is supremely wise, powerful, and loving so that we're no longer anxious in heart and no longer frantic in action. As I've said, it's living *from* fullness, not *for* fullness.

Many of us think we know this stuff, but we question its power. Be careful that you don't just have intellectual knowledge of it without the practiced, experiential reality of it. Be humble enough to be honest. When the truth of God's love becomes an experienced, embodied reality to you, you won't be as driven, fearful, and fragile! What an invitation—even for driven, exhausted, burdened leaders—to reset our souls every day by focusing on, recognizing, receiving, and resting in the Father's love. Practice these meta-skills until they become second nature. That's how you take the long road back.

> **When the truth of God's love becomes an experienced, embodied reality to you, you won't be as driven, fearful, and fragile!**

CHAPTER 7

BUILDING RESILIENT TEAMS

GREG'S TAKE

What makes a great organization? How can you have resilient, healthy teams?

Why do some thrive, some strive, some die?

A lot has been written on this subject. Chip will address it in depth, but I wanted to give a few observations.

When we started Seacoast, I'm not sure I could spell the word "culture." It just wasn't on my radar screen. Our team consisted of a bunch of volunteers and two full-time staff members, including me. Since I was new to the community and

THE ENDURANCE FACTOR

Sundays tended to come every seven days, I was consumed with message planning and sharing vision. There wasn't time to think about culture.

What I've since learned is that culture eats vision for breakfast. You can have a great vision, but if the culture isn't right, the team can implode with the first round of resistance or conflict. What I've discovered is that if you have more than one person on your team, you are going to have resistance, conflict, and communication issues. Count on it. Better yet, plan for it.

I've learned that there are at least four building blocks for great organizations:

- The right vision: Where are we going?
- The right strategy: How are we going to get there?
- The right team: Who is going with us?
- The right culture: What is the environment that will allow maximum success?

Culture in an organization refers to the shared values, beliefs, practices, and attitudes that shape the behavior of the people on the team. It is the underlying personality of an organization or church that defines how things are done, how decisions are made, and how people interact with each other.

Culture is important for several reasons. Firstly, it provides a sense of identity and purpose for the organization, which can motivate team members and help them to feel more connected to the mission. Secondly, it can help to attract and retain team members who share similar values and beliefs, which can lead to a more cohesive and productive team. Thirdly, a strong culture can help to align the behaviors of individuals with the goals of the organization, leading to more effective decision-making and better outcomes.

A positive and healthy culture can also foster innovation, creativity, and open communication, while a toxic culture can lead to high turnover, low morale, and poor performance. Therefore, it is important for organizations to actively cultivate a culture that supports their mission and values, and to regularly assess and adjust their culture to ensure that it remains healthy and effective.

> **A positive and healthy culture can foster innovation, creativity, and open communication.**

Let me give you a quick peek at how we approach culture at Seacoast. We have four cultural responsibilities that are probably not unique to us, but how we implement them may be. We want our team to know them, do them, and replicate them. First, I'll tell you what they are and then give a few examples of how we communicate them.

THE ENDURANCE FACTOR
FOUR CULTURAL RESPONSIBILITIES

1) Love God.

> "Jesus replied: 'You shall love the Lord your God with all
> your heart, and with all your soul, and with all your mind.'
> This is the first and greatest commandment."
> —Matthew 22:37-38, NIV

We've spent a good portion of this book emphasizing the importance of receiving God's love and recalibrating our perspective accordingly. You can't give what you don't have. You can't export what you haven't imported. Effective, life-giving ministry begins with understanding what God really thinks about you. He loves you. It's important to start there.

It's also important to respond to His love with what I call "an abiding sense of awe." The longer you are in vocational ministry, the easier it is to become a "professional." We start taking things for granted that once moved us with emotion. We get a behind-the-scenes view of "how the sausage is made" in the local church, and we may become jaded. We can lose that sense of awe that God actually lets us participate in His kingdom work.

I like to take time occasionally to just remember. Remember what? Remember the first time God used me to accomplish something only He could do.

I remember when I was an 18-year-old rockstar wannabe. What our band lacked in talent we made up for in volume. One night our band was asked to play at a large youth gathering in Chicago and there was an expectation to give an altar call at the end of the performance. Normally we would play our final song, walk off stage, stand behind the curtain, and hope that rousing applause would beckon one more curtain call. This night was different. One of us had to make a presentation of the gospel. The problem was that none of us were following Jesus all that closely. Our hearts were in the right place, but our actions sometimes lagged. The other band members volunteered me, based on the fact that my dad was a preacher. Reluctantly, I agreed and stumbled through a less than adequate—at least in my mind—presentation at the end of the concert.

I will never forget the sense of awe I felt when, not only did they listen, but dozens responded to the call. I called my girlfriend back in Denver that night (she's still my girlfriend, but now I'm married to her). I told her what had happened and how amazing it was. To be used by God was indescribable. I was in awe of the moment.

I don't ever want to lose that sense of awe that God would use me. You may want to stop and remember a time that God used you in a supernatural way. Remember how you felt. Don't lose it. Don't be a pro. Love God.

2) Treat people right.

> "And the second is like it: 'Love your neighbor as yourself.'"
> —Matthew 22:39, NIV

THE ENDURANCE FACTOR

Ministry can be tough. As we've previously discussed, Covid created a lot of uncertainty and stress. Some of us got into ministry because we loved people and sensed God's call. Then reality hits. Sheep are cute, fluffy creatures until you discover that they bite. Some of them have a taste for shepherds . . . and some are rabid.

I've heard it said jokingly that "ministry would be great if it wasn't for the people!" The problem is this: there would be no ministry if there weren't people. It's easy to get hurt and respond accordingly. It's been said, "Hurt people, hurt people." That's true not only of sheep but of shepherds. A mentor once told me that if you are going to be a good pastor, you've got to have thick skin and a tender heart. If you have thin skin and a hard heart, you'll never treat people the way they need to be treated. You will continue a never-ending, self-protecting cycle of abuse. That is especially true of your team.

Jesus made it simple in his response to someone who wanted to know which of His 613 commandments was the most important: "Love God and treat people right by loving them as you want to be loved."

When an honest conversation needs to happen, how would you want to be treated? When there is a discussion about compensation, how would you want to be treated? When there is a necessary ending, how would you want to be treated? Just treat people the way you would want them to treat you.

Paul the Apostle puts it in context of family:

> "Do not rebuke an older man harshly, but exhort him as if he were your father. Treat younger men as brothers, older women as mothers, and younger women as sisters, with absolute purity." —1 Timothy 5:1-2, NIV

We are a body, not a business; a family, not a corporation. If you treat people right, they will, more likely than not, return the favor.

3) Get better.

> "Let the wise listen and add to their learning, and let the discerning get guidance . . ." —Proverbs 1:5, NIV

The third cultural responsibility has to do with a personal commitment to becoming the best possible version of yourself. Proverbs says the wise "listen and add." In fact, I would argue that it's a continuous cycle of "listening and adding," getting better and better at whatever assignment that God has called you to. I want to be listening and learning how to do it better every day and on the last day, until I breathe my final breath.

We want to be a learning environment. We want our team to have a passion for getting better. It requires humility and hard work. Humility says, "I don't know it all. I'm capable of learning more, and I can learn from anyone if I just ask the right questions." Hard work involves figuring out what I need to learn and who can help me learn it.

THE ENDURANCE FACTOR

At a basic level, getting better is about reading the manuals, learning the craft, and putting in the time. At a deeper level, getting better is about finding people who are further down the road than you are and asking questions. At the deepest level, it's craving coaching. It's asking people to speak into your life and help you mine the hidden treasure that God has planted inside of you.

> Paul encouraged the Christians in Colossae, "Work willingly at whatever you do, as though you were working for the Lord rather than for people. Remember that the Lord will give you an inheritance as your reward, and that the Master you are serving is Christ." —Colossians 3:23-24, NLT

When the whole team buys into getting better, by God's grace, you'll be amazed at what's possible.

4) Maintain a good attitude.

> "Do everything without complaining and arguing."
> —Philippians 2:14, NLT

A negative attitude is the biggest threat to culture.

It's a fact: Things are difficult everywhere! Jesus said, "In this world you will have trouble" (John 16:33, NIV). Show me an organization where there is no tension and stress, and I'll show you an organization where nothing is getting done.

Show me an organization where there are no personality rubs, I'll show you an organization that has only one employee.

Show me an organization where everybody gets equal treatment, and I'll show you a graveyard.

Until your body is at room temperature, stuff will happen, deadlines will keep rushing toward you, and people will occasionally rub you wrong. If you have a bad attitude about it, you'll sabotage your own happiness and threaten the culture of your organization.

We need to see ourselves as thermostats, not thermometers. A thermometer reflects the temperature, a thermostat sets the temperature. We have a responsibility to set the temperature of every room we walk into, regardless of what the current circumstances are.

> **The key to a good attitude is a healthy dose of gratitude. When gratitude walks in, complaining and entitlement walks out.**

That's not easy. No one said it would be, but Paul seemed to think it was achievable. He doesn't say, "Do MOST things without complaining and arguing." He says "everything." "Do

THE ENDURANCE FACTOR

EVERYTHING without complaining and arguing" (Philippians 2:14, author paraphrase).

The key to a good attitude is a healthy dose of gratitude. When gratitude walks in, complaining and entitlement walks out. No wonder Paul exhorts us to:

> "Give thanks in all circumstances; for this is God's will for you in Christ Jesus." —1 Thessalonians 5:18, NIV

I can find something to complain about or give thanks for in every circumstance. I'm not a victim; I have a choice.

At Seacoast, we have very practical ways we communicate and reinforce the four responsibilities to build a great culture:

- We onboard each new team member with an understanding of their cultural responsibilities.
- We teach on one of the responsibilities at our all staff meeting each month.
- We give out a 'Youda' award (as in, "Youda man," "Youda woman") each month and year to the person who best reflects that month's values and responsibility.
- We make the cultural responsibilities a part of the employee review process.
- We use the cultural responsibilities as the baseline for difficult conversations.

As you can probably see, our cultural responsibilities are baked into our system.

That's because culture eats vision, and we want the vision to taste good.

CHIP'S TAKE

Do you have certain quotes that have been seeded in your soul for decades? They may come from books, or messages, or even just pop out in God-inspired conversation. I have several of them that are never far from my thoughts when I'm spending time with pastors, leaders, and their teams. One of them came from *EXECUTION: The Discipline of Getting Things Done* by Larry Bossily and Ram Charan. Here it is:

> *"The culture of an organization is the behavior of its leaders."*[25]

Reflect on that for a few moments. Here's another way to say it: *We teach what we know, but we reproduce who we are*—our character, our attitudes, our affections, our relationship style, and on and on. Let me put it the other way: The culture of any organization is shaped by the behaviors the leaders model, celebrate, and tolerate. Culture always settles to the level of the leader(s). Culture isn't found in carefully worded mission and vision statements, and it's not in a well-crafted strategy . . . it's in how leaders treat people.

Do you talk and teach about creating a "culture of honor?" Do you verbally champion phrases like, "Honor up, down, and all around?" Are the arrows of honor flowing equally in every

---

25 Larry Bossily and Ram Charan, *EXECUTION: The Discipline of Getting Things Done* (New York: Random House, 2009), p. 89.

direction and of equal weight, or is there an unspoken reality that *honoring up* is the most important thing in your world? Honor is communicated in our use of two of our most limited, and therefore, most valuable possessions: time and attention. We each have a painfully limited amount of each. When we invest our time and attention in another person, we're communicating honor. But people need both—we can give time without attention, but we can't give attention without time. In other words, we can be in the room with someone but not be emotionally present. Most leaders are good communicators, but they're not automatically great listeners. If we want to build cultures that honor up, down, and all around, we all need to cultivate better listening skills. It matters. It matters a lot. People feel valued when they feel heard, and really hearing someone requires being present with them.

> **When we invest our time and attention in another person, we're communicating honor.**

More than one pastor has confided to me, "I don't know what's wrong with our team. Very few of them bring any new ideas or engage in robust dialogue to find better ways to do things. It's frustrating. They're not "showing up" fully and helping drive the vision." That reminds me of a concept I got from another book, *Enlightened Leadership*, by Ed Oakley and Doug Krug. In the book, they ask the question, "Do you have a *TELL* culture or an *ASK* culture?"[26] I've found it to be a really helpful lens to look at your leadership style. Do you lead meetings with the leaders of your team by TELLING them what the organization needs and how to get it, or do you lead these meetings by ASKING questions that help them DISCOVER what the organization needs and how to go about accomplishing it. Questions invite reflection and thought. Questions (and listening to the answers) honor the time and intellect of the other people. When a leader tells what he thinks on the front end of a meeting or conversation, it's no longer a discussion. Your team believes that one critical component of their job description is to get you what you want. When you *tell* them what you want, they see no need to be creative or even think about alternatives. As you are going into a meeting, ask yourself, "Am I creating an environment for declaration or an environment of discovery?"

If you want to create an environment for discovery that stimulates your people to think more creatively, write a question or a challenge at the top of a large whiteboard and then leave the room. Before walking out, tell them, "I'll be back in thirty minutes. I want the board to be full of ideas." When you come back, don't tell them their ideas are stupid. Affirm each person, even if only because they took the risk of voicing an idea. You can

---

26 Ed Oakley and Doug Krug, *Enlightened Leadership* (New York: Fireside, 1991).

say, "Let's filter through these and find the gems." When you begin discussing them, put a piece of duct tape over your mouth. You'll have the last word, but you need to realize that *your first word is the last word.* After you've read the ideas on the whiteboard, let others bat the ideas around. Just nod and smile. Will this take time? Yes, of course, but if you want to develop leaders who can think, and stimulate creativity and ownership of plans, you have to give them a safe place to practice. You don't have to do anything they suggest but empowering them to explore and discover ideas and then listening to them creates a culture of honor that draws the best out of them.

Let's talk about what I believe is the elephant in the room when it comes to discipling followers of Jesus and developing leaders for His church. Discipling believers and developing leaders both work best in a life-on-life, caught-more-than-taught, "be-with-Him" kind of process. It's slower and messier. It's not sexy or showy. Let me offer three suggestions as you ponder your strategy to make disciples and build leaders:

- "Less is more." If you focus on fewer people and invest more time in connecting with them, building relationships, and developing their gifts and abilities, you will have a greater return on your investment than if you focus on a lot of people with less personal contact and virtually no relationship building. Not only do you identify and develop their potential, but you also win their hearts by loving them enough to give your two most valuable possessions: time and attention. Friends don't leave friends.

- "Slow is fast." No argument from me—this is a slower way to build and develop your team, but in the long run, you create a culture of honor, you earn higher levels of loyalty, and you avoid a continual cycle of short-term staff that you often need to hire and replace. This enables you and your team to avoid the stress of the interruptions experienced when key players leave, and new ones have to be oriented to your organization.

- "Deep is wide." When you develop a culture that's more like a family than a factory, you enjoy rich benefits. When relationships are built through time and talk, when it's easy, and when it's hard, the sense of family and belonging goes to another level that few ever experience. It encourages people to develop deep roots in the community, and it produces a matrix of life and leadership you create together. The influence and impact that you collectively carry gives greater reach, and the community you build has greater depth.

Team members look to the pastor or their immediate leader from three perspectives. One is spiritual. One is practical. And one is psychological. We need to be aware of the tricky mixed drink this can make. Greg has talked in earlier chapters about your identity, your calling, and your assignment. The spiritual perspective is seeing your role in the organization as your assignment from God. The practical perspective is that this is my J.O.B. It's how I feed my family, and I want to fulfill my role to the best of my ability. The third perspective, the psychological, is often where it gets tricky. Virtually all of us arrive on a team with unresolved, unprocessed, and unhealed wounds from all the experiences we've had up to that point. Our number one need is to be loved, valued, and feel a sense of belonging. Team members often look to their leaders to make up for what life hasn't provided up to that point. They often look to their pastor as a kind of father figure, whether they realize it or not. They crave the pastor's approval. . . . they need it like they need their next breath. Being a father figure complicates relationships quite a bit! People who had difficult relationships with their dads usually bring those perceptions to their working relationships, so they may be adversely affected by the pastor's personality or behavior. Because they're looking to the leader to meet a need that the leader's not responsible for meeting, it can cause some awkward and unhealthy cycles. I've found it helpful to make this concept an integral part of training a team. Teach and talk openly about how past relationships affect us. It's normal, but not helpful, to project onto the people in our lives right now the qualities other key figures from our past modeled and the responsibilities in which they failed us. When we engage these issues openly, it makes it an element of our relational culture that can be more naturally explored and dealt with.

You're going to build your team one of two ways: You're either going to develop talent or hire it. As we discussed earlier, each one has different challenges. If you want to develop talent, it'll take more of your time and energy, and it'll be slower. You'll be frustrated because whatever you delegate you could do faster and better. But if you patiently develop and delegate, there's a big upside: you'll eventually have someone who shares your heart, enhances the culture, and has a trusting relationship with you. This process is short-term slow but long-term fast—when you build people for the team, they're more creative, more committed to each other, more dedicated to mutual accountability instead of only top-down, and more enthusiastic in seeing the shared vision become a reality, so things can happen more quickly than if you had to manage a variety of expectations.

Hiring talent is a different animal. It's about finding the right set of gifts and talent, often by using external incentives. The new hires may shine for a while in their specific role, but have they caught your culture? We all agree that "Culture trumps vision." Do you remember that when you're building your team? Culture is a reflection of who you are on the inside, not what you do on the outside. Those who are hired from outside, especially if they're superstars, are wired to create culture that reflects who they are, not to be integrated into an existing culture. I'm not saying you should never hire from outside your organization. I'm stressing that you should be very mindful of the unique challenges that come with it.

The key to creating a healthy team, a healthy church, and a healthy family is to pursue your own health. There's no shortcut, and there's no alternative. All (yes, all) burned out leaders I've ever known failed to prioritize personal thriving, so they were poor models for those close to them. As they began sliding toward the red line, they ignored the warning signs, rationalizing to keep running at 100 mph, and blaming others who slowed them down.

> **The key to creating a healthy team, a healthy church, and a healthy family is to pursue your own health. There's no shortcut, and there's no alternative.**

When I talk to someone who is on the slippery slope to burnout, I ask a question that often surprises them: "What does it take for you to feel good about yourself when you wake up in the morning?" If it's how many and how much, who says nice things about you, and how many likes you get on your social media page, you're on the wrong road. It's so easy to get your agenda out of whack. Everything in our world, and too often in our church world, screams that our value as leaders comes from our production, especially compared to *that* church and *that* leader. Accomplishments feel good for a while, but they can never give us the fulfillment we crave. Our security never comes from numbers, fame, or likes; it comes from our position as people who bask in the Father's strong love. (Yes, I know we've covered this before, but it's easy to miss it.)

There's nothing wrong with *wanting* your church to grow and have kingdom impact, but we get in trouble when we *need* it to grow larger and have a greater impact than someone else's church. If that's our identity, we'll be puffed up with pride when we're doing better than someone else, we'll always worry that we're falling behind, we'll always resent those who are getting ahead of us, and we'll feel self-pity because we've worked so hard and nobody really appreciates us. How do we determine if something we're feeling is a want or a need? A need is something or someone whose absence makes us sick, but restoration heals us, and a consistent supply keeps us healthy. Then, when *our wants* are blocked, we're disappointed, but not crushed. Their restoration gives us relief and joy, and their consistent presence lifts our soul. But when *our needs* are blocked, it affects us in much more profound ways. We're heartsick, defiant or depressed, furious or frantic, neurotic or nasty.

What does all this have to do with creating resilient teams? Everything! If we reproduce who we are, then our people need us to receive and rest in the Father's love so that our relationships with them are an overflow of that love.

As I watch leaders and meet with them, I have a very simple filtering question: Can I picture Jesus saying what they're saying and doing what they're doing the way they're saying and doing it? He was authentic and appropriate in every setting. He was amazingly kind and patient with those who struggle, including the guys who followed Him for years but remained so clueless; but when the Pharisees harmed the people He loved, He called them out. He didn't say corrective things to punish them, but to call them to repent. Truth and grace, all day every day. As leaders, our task is to represent, or maybe better, re-present Jesus to the people who cross our paths, and especially those who are close to us. This means we need to be sensitive to the Father's leading before, during, and after conversations. Even Jesus relied on the Father for insight about His relationships. He said, "I don't speak on my own authority. The Father who sent me has commanded me what to say and how to say it" (John 12:49, NLT), and "I tell you the truth, the Son can do nothing by himself. He does only what he sees the Father doing. Whatever the Father does, the Son also does" (John 5:19, NLT). That's our measuring stick: Do our words and actions, publicly and privately, reflect the Father and Jesus?

> **Jesus respected His disciples and His listeners enough to speak the truth without a shred of manipulation — no masks, no games, just truth spoken with love.**

I'm not advocating that leaders become placid like the stained-glass Jesus with the lamb on His shoulders. Jesus was

GREG SURRATT AND CHIP JUDD

both the Lamb of God and the Lion of Judah. He was kind most of the time and fierce when He needed to be. He wasn't naïve about people, but He wasn't a cynic either. Anyone who called a Rome-allied tax collector and a zealot to follow Him must have had a phenomenal ability to bring very different people together on a cohesive team! Intensity wasn't wrong for Jesus, and it's not wrong for us, but it needs to be energized by the love of God, not the desire to dominate. Jesus respected His disciples and His listeners enough to speak the truth without a shred of manipulation—no masks, no games, just truth spoken with love.

Your influence doesn't stop with your words. Your content is important, but your ethos (the fundamental character behind your words) and pathos (the emotion, empathy, and compassion present in your words) communicate even more powerfully. The people around you are looking for someone to trust even more than for someone to lead. Do the hard but necessary work to become secure in God's great love, forgiveness, and acceptance, and then treat people the way God is treating you.

CHAPTER 8

IT'S (ALMOST) NEVER TOO LATE

GREG'S TAKE

My grandson Miles plays soccer. He's good, having recently been chosen for the All-Region team as just an eighth grader playing varsity for his high school. One weekend, when he was younger, I took him to a game while his parents were away. I asked him, "Miles, how many goals are you going to score for Papa today?"

He had scored five goals the previous week.

After thinking about it, he announced, "Papa, I'm going to score two goals for you."

THE ENDURANCE FACTOR

That weekend the coach needed him to play defense, so he didn't score any goals. They won the game, and he played quite well. On the way home, I told him how proud I was of him, and he responded, "Papa, I didn't play well. I said I was going to score two goals and I didn't score any."

His response was like a red light that went off in my soul. I had asked him to take responsibility in an area where he had no authority. That's a sure-fire definition for stress. On defense, he couldn't control how many goals he scored. (And even on offense, he can't control his opportunities to score.) All he could control was the hustle and effort he put into playing the game.

I've never asked him or any of our other grandkids that question again. I only ask them if they're going to hustle and give it their best. That's all they can control.

My life verse speaks so clearly to this issue: "Let us not become weary in doing good, for at the proper time we will reap a harvest if we do not give up" (Galatians 6:9, NIV).

Are you discouraged? Are you weary? You're not alone. It's a common theme in leadership. If it wasn't, Paul wouldn't have written about it.

Sometimes we may need to reassess our assignment—Chip will talk about that more in this chapter—but often the root cause of our discouragement is that we're taking responsibility in areas over which we have no authority. In other words, we're trying to control things that we have no ability to control.

My responsibility is to do good. What does that look like?

- Good is creating patterns and systems that promote spiritual, mental, and relational health—and sticking with them.
- Good is digging deep into your identity as God's beloved child. Let that soak into the crevasses of your heart so that it permeates every thought, word, and action.
- Good is making the hard but necessary choices to create new rhythms for yourself, your family, and your leadership role.

Your life and your legacy depend on it.

> Sometimes we may need to reassess our assignment—often the root cause of our discouragement is that we're taking responsibility in areas over which we have no authority.

God's responsibilities are the things that pastors normally stress over: The size and timing of the harvest. You and I have no control over that. My grandson Miles couldn't control how many goals he scored. There were too many variables involved. It's the same with leading a church.

There is a promise here, however: If you and I will focus on our part (doing good), and trust that God will do His part, you can be sure the harvest is coming. You can't control when it will happen, or how large it will be, but you know that God is true to His word, and the harvest will come. He promised it. At just the right time.

We usually end our retreats with a challenge. On the last day, I want those who attend to get alone with God in nature and ask themselves two questions:

- What am I going to take home from our experience together?
- What am I going to leave at the table?

It's always an emotional time that evening as we share our reflections on the week. The friendships are almost always the number one takeaway that we so desperately need and have watched develop over such a short time. It's those relationships—Chip calls it *a brotherhood*—that are the first endurance factors that are key to living well and finishing strong. The importance of rest is another. Some say that their takeaway is renewed vision, and others point to a fresh passion to see themselves as God sees them: beloved sons and daughters of the Creator.

They often say they're leaving behind their insecurity, their constant striving to be good enough, their frenetic schedules, or their gnawing self-doubts.

We end the night by reading a poem that feels more like a Psalm. "The Table," written by my friend Jonathan Wiggins,[27] carries his reflections of what happens when wounded, broken warriors gather around the table of healing and hope:

It is no small thing to convene here. Each of us possessors/carriers of influence, vision, grit and wisdom have momentarily entrusted our life's work into the hands of those we have trained and empowered. We have gathered from different locations, backgrounds and have taken very different journeys in every respect to be here. Still, all have arrived at this place.

This retreat. This table.

It is no small thing.

Around this table we choose to take time to be together. Here we voluntarily and collectively unburden ourselves bit by bit. We understand it takes time for a man to break free from the urgent, unimportant things in his life. It always takes time.

We laugh loud together at this table. We feast like kings here. We take chances here. We win and lose here. We choose trust here. Each of us is better in some way because we are here.

This is no ordinary table. It is bigger than the room it occupies. It's corners are growing. It is a table of influence that has been built for leaders. Built for kings.

---

27 Jonathan Wiggins, "The Table," used by permission.

THE ENDURANCE FACTOR

It is like King Solomon's table. Solomon would influence the known world in his day as kings and queens of the earth would sit at his table to break bread with him and to inquire of his wisdom and of his God.

It is like the table dreamt of by Dr. Martin Luther King JR. This dream was conceived in the mind of a man who was a King by virtue of both his name and his conduct rather than his position or office. Still, this King would impact the course of history. His legacy still does. Reverend King spoke of his dream one sunny, dry day on August 28, 1963 on the mall in Washington DC when he prophesied, "I have a dream that one day on the red hills of Georgia the sons of former slaves and the sons of former slave owners will be able to sit together at the table of brotherhood."

This is no ordinary table.

It is like King David's table. This ancient leader. This Poet-Warrior, Shepherd-King would capture the essential character of his God by writing the words, "You prepare a table before me in the presence of my enemies."

Just as God prepared tables for King David, King Solomon, Dr King and other great kings who have gone before us, He has done the same for this still-forming band of brothers. God prepared this table, this retreat and this moment for a motley crew, an unlikely, blended

*family made up of warriors, shepherds, romantics,
poets, kings and sages.*

It is no small thing to gather around this table.

*God has prepared it only for those whose lives will
in some way impact the course of history.*

God has prepared this table for you.

CHIP'S TAKE

I want to wrap up my part of this last chapter by sharing a couple of thoughts on why pastors and leaders self-sabotage, and too, how to look at difficult moments as gifts or opportunities on our journey to achieve our full potential. The obvious event, issue, or behavior that brings a leader down is never the fundamental problem. It's the fruit, not the root. It's the proverbial tip of the iceberg. The issues that made the pastor or leader, who is probably a good-hearted and competent person, vulnerable to the bad decisions that took them off course are deeper and tied to unmet needs, unprocessed pain, and unhealed wounds from his or her past.

In an earlier chapter, we discovered that meeting a right need the wrong way is at the bottom of every sin cycle. It's having a thirst in our souls that we've never learned how to quench, but instead, we've developed unhealthy, unholy ways to experience counterfeit satisfaction of that need being met. Often, those unhealthy and unholy ways of getting our needs met destroy our reputation and our career, but they are almost never the real story of the person's identity and character. The real story is the deep need that's never been met correctly and sufficiently for which they've developed grossly unhealthy methods to medicate.

I began following the Lord at twenty-three, one month after I got married to my awesome wife, Coleen. I was raised as an *American heathen*. We never went to church, and I wasn't raised with a sense of God and His ways. I was a teenager during the late 60s and early 70s. I enjoyed all that that time had to offer in the form of drug, sex, and rock 'n' roll. I had a problem with pornography, cheated on every person I ever dated, and partied with abandon. My psychosexual script of how intimacy between a man and a woman works came from a perverted business run by ungodly men. I battled with lust for several years, even after being married and saved. It would've been easy to say I was a sexual deviant, particularly from a Christian perspective.

As I walked out my own journey of healing and have since worked with many, many men struggling in these areas, I've learned the diagnosis and treatment for what ails us is usually not as simple and easy as we like to make it. From working through my childhood experiences, I realized that I didn't know how to create and enjoy true intimacy. I had "attachment issues," which means that I didn't know how to form a deep emotional attachment to another person. My thirst for intimacy went unquenched, and I learned to medicate the thirst with sex. Sex gave me a temporary, powerful, counterfeit substitute for my thirst. I could feel connected and excited by the game of attraction and the experience of sex. As God kindly and patiently led me toward healing, I realized that my real issue was not sexual. My issue was a wounded soul that felt lonely and unattached. As I learned to connect deeply to God and His love, His love transferred over to my relationship with myself, my wife, my children, and others. As I learned to experience and enjoy deeper intimacy in a healthy way, my struggles with my sexuality shrunk at a rate I never expected. I thought I would struggle with those issues at that level for the rest of my life.

The reason we often don't get free from persistent sin and struggle is we're attacking the fruit and strengthening the root. If all self-sabotaging sin cycles are driven by our attempts to meet a right need the wrong way, then it seems obvious that the way to break those cycles is to identify the need and learn a healthy way to meet the need. If we deal only with the behavior that got us in trouble, we are dealing with the fruit of the cycle. When we slow down and work through earlier, developmental stages of life, we often identify the unmet need, the root, and then we can establish healthy patterns to meet that need.

Far too often, Greg and I deal with pastors and leaders who have fallen into trouble by focusing on the sinful behavior and applying discipline to that alone. They need to engage in the slower, harder work of identifying the unmet need and how it led them to the unhealthy behavior. For those of us who are trying to help them, if we deal with the behavior and fail to break the cycle driven by the unmet need, the cycle will repeat itself by finding another counterfeit source to temporarily medicate the pain of the unmet need. It's trading one poisonous root for another.

> **Don't waste your pain! The best way to avoid wasting pain is to learn from it.**

You might want to yell at me, "Dude, what are you trying to tell me?"

Simply this: Don't waste your pain! The best way to avoid wasting pain is to learn from it. Ask it what it's trying to tell you about yourself. When a relationship gets off track, when a plan falls short of your expectations, when you repeat destructive behavior that you've tried to stop many times, when you're hurt and disappointed by how other people treat you, when you're totally confused by doing a self-destructive and relationally harmful thing again, are you willing to ask one of the most important questions you can ask?

God, what are you trying to show me about me?

Trouble works for you. It is on your payroll. Check out this thought from 2 Corinthians 4:17-18: "For our momentary, light affliction is producing for us an eternal weight of glory far beyond all comparison, while we look not at the things which are seen, but at the things which are not seen; for the things which are seen are temporal, but the things which are not seen are eternal." You can blame it on the devil, on other people, or on unforeseen circumstances, but we have to admit that at least a portion of the heartache we suffer is self-inflicted. Some of us have a default setting that it's *never* our fault, so we look for ways to blame people or God, but others live with a default setting that it's *always* their fault, so they constantly beat themselves bloody with self-condemnation. The leaders that come to me are coming because something's wrong. They have found themselves in some form of "trouble." It has been my honor to help pastors and leaders see that God is always working on them, in them, through them, and around them to make them into the person He sees in them, and then take them into the destiny He has waiting for them. God has given me a cool perspective of John 15:2 that has helped many struggling pastors and leaders. Jesus told His disciples, "I am the true grapevine, and my Father is the gardener. He cuts off every branch of mine that *doesn't* produce fruit, and he prunes the branches that *do bear fruit* so they will *produce even more*" (John 15:1-2, NLT emphasis mine). It's been my observation that most of us misinterpret or misapply this verse. What's actually happening here? If you *haven't* born fruit, God tells you to go sit in the corner until you're ready to get in the game. If you *have* borne fruit, He uses various means to make you aware of areas in which He wants to make adjustments in you and to you that will enable you to bear more fruit in the seasons to come. But many of us have missed the point of the passage: When God is pruning a person, it's one of the highest compliments He can give you. He's saying, "You have produced fruit. I'm pleased with that, and I have more for you to do. To prepare you for the next season of more fruitfulness, I need to develop you in certain areas that will serve you well where I want to take you. So, if you submit to My loving work, you will become a man or woman that can walk into the future I've planned for you." In effect, in these painful moments, God is saying, "Hey, my beloved son (or daughter), I love what you've done for the kingdom, and I have more for you. To get there, you need to work on some things. I'm pruning you because I love you and see more potential in you, not because I'm disappointed in you. Some attitudes and behaviors that weren't big roadblocks at this level would be huge hindrances at the next level. This pruning is designed to draw you closer to Me and make you even more useful to the kingdom." (That's the Chip Standard Version.)

What are some things that God prunes in us? Maybe the realization of the effects of our anger, our impatience with people, our neglect of our personal health, our exceedingly rapid pace, past resentments we thought we'd buried but keep affecting us, our misguided agenda to promote our own fame, our compulsion to try to control the size of the harvest, mixing up our wants and needs, and secret sins we've hidden for years. A sure sign of spiritual maturity is the ability to see God's gracious and strong hand in the midst of trouble.

When we go through times of pruning, we need to reinforce the four meta-skills: find a band of brothers or sisters where you can be vulnerable and receive support, develop a conversational relationship with God through journaling, keep your emotional bucket filled by going to God first and most for everything you need, and become skilled at killing your ANTs.

> **A sure sign of spiritual maturity is the ability to see God's gracious and strong hand in the midst of trouble.**

Now, at the end of this book, I want to talk specifically to different kinds of readers:

- You may be doing pretty well. Your marriage is strong, your kids know you cherish them, your team feels encouraged and well-led, and your schedule reflects God's priorities in your life. (I'm glad both of you read our book!) God probably wants you to reach out to some of your peers to help them move toward living well, avoiding burnout, and finishing strong. Build a band of brothers, and create a culture of grace, truth, and time.

THE ENDURANCE FACTOR

- You may be too dedicated to ministry growth, and your family isn't getting your best. Your spouse feels abandoned, or at least like a fifth wheel, and your kids are angry at you and the church for taking you away from them. Consider significant changes you could make to restore what your hyper-drive for success has harmed. Your family cares more about you making the family a priority than they do your success; they crave your presence with them—physically and emotionally—so they're assured that you adore them. Your family life is the launching pad for your credibility as a leader. Misplaced priorities always cost a lot. We can pay a little now, or we can pay a lot more later. Be smart and make the changes today.

- You may be struggling with anxiety, depression, and burnout. See a specialist and discover the cause. Your emotions and your physical health are one of the ways God will communicate with you. If you're not living by healthy rhythms, you'll suffer consequences sooner or later. Don't wait for a crisis to start examining how you're doing on the inside. You'll need help discovering where and why you continue following cycles that hurt you and the ones you love. Get the help you need.

- You may be thinking about quitting. Find a wise, competent friend or counselor to help you sort through it all. Is it an issue of identity, calling, or a changing of assignment? Is God using "trouble" to get your attention? Was there a wrong turn in the past that led you to this point? Are you at the wrong place at the wrong time? Is your calling secure but your assignment isn't working? These situations are almost always quite complex. Which is why we need someone from the outside to look at what's going on objectively and offer a range of options. . . . and yes, there are always multiple options.

Now, at the end of the book, if you got nothing else from Greg and me, I hope you've been prompted to spend the rest of your life with the primary focus of recognizing, receiving, and resting in the Father's love. Without that, you'll be insecure, driven, or passive. With it, you'll have a beautiful and powerful experience of your identity as His child and your infinite worth and value in His eyes. Your life will be richer in ways you can't even imagine.

ABOUT THE AUTHORS

GREG SURRATT is the founding pastor of Seacoast Church, which he planted with a small group of like-minded people in 1988. Together, they made 16,000 phone calls to people in the area to better understand what they look for in a church. Today, Seacoast has a dozen campuses throughout South Carolina and North Carolina, as well as a thriving online community.

Over the past several years, Greg has grown increasingly concerned with the mental health of pastors, with studies showing as many as 42% of them are in various stages of burnout. In 2018, Greg founded The Pastors Collective to address this growing crisis, and opened The Retreat at Church Creek in 2021 to provide a refuge for pastors to rest and make lasting connections with others.

THE ENDURANCE FACTOR

Greg is a co-founder of the Association of Related Churches (ARC), which is a global church-planting initiative that has established over 1,000 churches worldwide since its founding in 2000. He is the author of the books *IR-REV-REND*, *Re-visioning*, and *The Endurance Factor*, as well as a contributor to various podcasts and magazines.

Greg is married to his childhood sweetheart, Debbie, and together they have four children and fourteen grandchildren. He enjoys photography, fishing, golfing, and rooting for the Cubs, Broncos, and Gamecocks.

CHIP JUDD is the Pastor of Leadership Care at Seacoast Church in Charleston, SC, where he invests in the health and development of the staff and campus pastors. He is honored to work under Greg and Josh Surratt to help leaders "Live Well and Finish Strong."

He is also the Founder of MorphQuest, a 501(c)(3) through which he counsels, coaches, and consults with individuals, leaders, and organizations helping them to identify, challenge, and change their counterproductive patterns of thought, belief, or behavior.

Chip has been in pastoral ministry for over forty-three years and counseling has been a large part of his ministry from the beginning. He received his Master's in Counseling at The Citadel and started a counseling practice in addition to continuing to pastor. Chip's counseling and pastoring experience combine to give him unique and powerful insight into blind spots and blockages in marriages, families, churches, and their ministry teams. He seeks to present Biblical truth mixed with "sanctified psychology" to bring about real freedom and lasting change.

Chip and Coleen have been married for forty-seven years and have three married adult children, two great sons-in-law, a great daughter-in-law, and seven amazing grandchildren.

THE RETREAT AT CHURCH CREEK

The Retreat at Church Creek is a refuge for pastors who feel alone, burned out, or just need some rest and to recharge.

The Retreat is located on sixty-six acres, just thirty minutes from the airport and thirty minutes from downtown Charleston and is owned and operated by The Pastors Collective non-profit.

The retreat center property includes a fourteen-acre freshwater bass lake, a dock on deep water that is just minutes from the intercoastal waterway and the Atlantic Ocean, two miles of peaceful trails, a gun range, hot tub, and fire pits.

The retreat center lodge sleeps eighteen people with six-and-a-half baths. Programming for The Retreat at Church

Creek is anchored by four-day retreats for up to fifteen pastors at a time.

Each retreat may include salt and freshwater fishing, disc golf, nature trails, access to an in-house fitness center (with coaching), cornhole, crazy ping pong, great conversations, and lots of relaxation.

At night, attendees and staff will share a great meal together and even greater discussions. At the end of the four days, participants will walk away with new friendships, resources, and ongoing support for those who would like to be involved in deeper soul care.

The Pastors Collective (https://pastorscollective.org/) is a non-profit founded by Pastor Greg Surratt in Charleston, South Carolina. The mission of The Pastors Collective is to provide opportunities to address the real and difficult work of planting, pastoring, and leading churches by fostering soul care, developing resources for pastors, and continuing a national dialogue on mental health in ministry.

THE AVAIL PODCAST

HOSTED BY VIRGIL SIERRA

AVAIL
PODCAST